# TOUCH MY BLOOD

FRED KHUMALO

# Touch My Blood
*The early years*

**UMUZI**

Published by Umuzi, P.O. Box 6810, Roggebaai 8012
an imprint of Random House (Pty) Ltd, Isle of Houghton,
Corner Boundary Road & Carse O'Gowrie, Houghton 2198, South Africa
Copyright © Fred Khumalo 2006
Fred Khumalo hereby asserts his right to be identified as the author of this work.
First edition, first printing 2006
ISBN: 1-4152-0004-1
Edited by Mike Nicol
Cover design by Abdul Amien
Cover photograpgh by Cedric Nunn
Design and layout by Nazli Jacobs
Set in Century Schoolbook
Printed and bound by Paarl Print, Oosterland Street, Paarl, South Africa

"My whole life has been an attempt to make myself a skeleton in my own cupboard."

DAMBUDZO MARECHERA.

# Contents

Prologue                                    9

Grandpa                                     15
Ubaba                                       26
Umama                                       29
Mpumalanga                                  42
Chickens for Africa                         47
Bewitched                                   56
Fever                                       71
Soccer wars                                 75
Two donkeys and an ass                      80
Mashicila                                   82
Bewitched again                             87
Piwe's cultural weapon                      89
A dangerous corpse                          100
Stingy Arab no more                         104
Life with the American Dudes                110
Nkawana is dead                             113
The going gets tough                        117
Mafika, my guru                             120
An accidental ringleader                    124
Pick up the spear                           128
Drinking from the forbidden well            133
The house on the hill                       138
A state of emergency                        144
Nkehli                                      148

We are watching you!                       152

An indecent proposal                    156

*Cosmopolitan* here I come!          160

The making of a killer               164

Whites only                            167

Debauchery at Snake Park         170

Writing or fighting?                  174

Falling in love again                181

Give us guns, not newspaper reports   185

Epilogue                            194

# Prologue

IT SURELY MUST BE THE PERFECT WAY to maim or silence an adversary in a crowded place without attracting attention. With the single-mindedness of a pervert and the casual air of a baker kneading dough, you reach out and grab his testicles and squeeze. He is so shocked he doesn't fight back. He's at your mercy, paralysed, his arms dangling.

This is not the sort of instruction you find in manuals on self-defence. It's something that happens on the spur of the moment, the result of an explosion of anger. Also, it's not a method to be proud of. Yet at the age of twenty-four, I found myself in a packed nightclub squeezing a man's balls.

In 1991 I was an intern on a programme run by the Canadian International Development Agency. The motivation was to help young black South Africans study and gain hands-on working experience with relevant institutions overseas.

I ended up in Canada. And on the night in question was with my fellow interns at the African Club, a haunt for African expatriates in Ottawa. We were relaxed and enjoying ourselves and eventually were introduced to a South African who had been in the country a long time. We were overjoyed, believing he would be our guide in this strange land.

"So, you guys tell me you from home, huh?" There was a slight twang to his voice. "Now, say this to me, why are black people fighting against each other seeing that the white man is ready to give them back power and land?"

Above the din of the music we tried to explain the complex political situation at home. When ANC supporters killed supporters of the Azanian People's Organisation, yet both organisations claimed to be fighting for black liberation, you were bound to be confused. Add the Inkatha Freedom Party to the equation, you were bound to lose whoever you were trying to enlighten on the intricacies of South African politics.

In response to our explanations our newly-discovered brother said, "Maybe the white man should continue oppressing our people if liberation is going to throw the country into civil war, know what I'm sayin'? Every time the white man grants black people their freedom in Africa they start fighting, you know what I'm sayin'?"

The tension was palpable. I tried to change the subject. "How is life treating you here? Any opportunities for the likes of us?"

"What do you think you have to offer us?"

Us? And then came the clincher. "So, how's Soweto now? Have the boers finally installed electricity into your houses or are you still using coal stoves and candles?"

Shock jolted through the dimly-illuminated faces around the table. Our compatriot didn't look much older than any of us. He couldn't have been born in exile, judging by his very South African accent and complete lack of political savvy.

Surely, no matter how long he had been in Canada or anywhere in the world for that matter, he must have seen the electrified houses, shops and streets of Soweto on TV, as the township had been the focus of the international media since the 1976 uprisings?

The man broke into my thoughts. "Am I right, then, to say that you guys in Soweto and the rest of black South Africa are still lagging behind, moving around in darkness . . ."

One of my colleagues stood up with a clenched fist, but I restrained him. I leaned towards our friend. Underneath the table, my right hand reached for his balls. I grabbed and squeezed viciously.

"Did you just say we are uncivilised black people wallowing in darkness?" I said between clenched teeth.

After what seemed like an eternity, I let go. The guy fell forward, his head hitting the top of the table. I pushed him off his chair and he fell to the floor.

By now I was spitting venom. My colleagues gently directed me to another corner of the club, away from the fool.

This is the unfortunate reality of a ghetto mentality – in our impotence and rage, we deride each other. I am a better kaffir because I am lighter than you. I am a better kaffir because I live in a house with running water and electricity. I am a better kaffir because I drive a better car than yours. I am a better kaffir because I went to school and you didn't.

We were still laughing at the ball-clenching incident when trouble walked in our direction. It came in the form of a matronly woman who had her brown hair tied in a bun. She was in her early fifties, accompanied by a girl and a young man. They'd apparently witnessed the incident. Could they be management? Were we in trouble?

Their accents gave them away as French-speakers. Alarm turned to relief when we learned that they were merely looking for fun. They joined us, and we started drinking merrily. I sat next to the woman whose name was Genevieve. The younger woman was her teenage daughter. The three were voyeurs who liked "mixing with the Africans".

"We love ze Africans. We come to Africa one day, we look you up, huh?"

"Oui, oui, my cherie," I assured her.

"Ze Africans are spiritual, deep people. That why I relate better to zem. Westerners are too, eh, plastic, huh?"

"Oui."

Her English wasn't good and occasionally, in frustration, she would lapse into her native French. The French phrases that I knew had drowned in the night's rivers of alcohol. The only one that stayed afloat and tempted use was *Je t'aime*, I love you. However, I felt it would be impudent to rush into that territory.

As the night reached its perfect maturity, as the tongues continued to wag freely, my right hand, cold from holding a beer glass all evening, made its first foray to the warm insides of Genevieve's thighs, encountering no resistance.

The following morning I woke in her bed. I had a headache so severe it felt as if my brain had been sprinkled with seeds of hot pepper and doused with Tabasco sauce.

Before I left we made love again. And then I walked out into the teeth of the winter morning air which bit my face ferociously until tears

11

TOUCH MY BLOOD

brimmed in my eyes. I quickened my pace, glad when I soon reached the hotel.

I had received a warm welcome to Canada. But despite this sense of satisfaction, the ball-clenching incident weighed heavily on my conscience. It was so out of character. Clearly I needed to deal with the demons from my past.

I was a young journalist who had found himself in the maw of a monster called violence. In the dying years of apartheid, black people who held conflicting political beliefs fought and killed each other. I had recorded numerous bloody scenes of political violence. Each side of the conflict had its favourite methods of killing its enemies. Supporters of Inkatha used assegais, guns and knobkerries. Supporters of the United Democratic Front/African National Congress preferred the necklace.

During my coverage of the political violence it wasn't uncommon for me to interview a widow about the death of her husband and her sons while the blood was still wet on the floor, while her tears of anguish still flowed, while the remains of her razed house still smouldered. After every job, I was overcome by the anger and shame of preying on other people's grief.

I had tried to keep a count of the dead bodies I had seen. This was a futile exercise. There were just too many. Writing about human beings, especially dead, or terrified, or angry human beings, takes a lot out of you. It's even worse if your own life is constantly under threat.

By coming to Canada I thought I had made a break with that sad past. Not so.

About a week later I stood at the window of my apartment in downtown Toronto, marvelling at the flakes of wind-driven snow. The wind shrieked, clawing my window. It was early in the morning. Below in Dundas Street East men dressed in heavy coats made their way to work.

Memories and questions flooded my mind. Again the ball-clenching incident surfaced. Was it just coincidence that violence always followed me wherever I went? Was I like Shakespeare's spirits ". . . doom'd for a certain term to walk the night . . ."? By township standards, I was

12

mild-mannered. But no matter how I chose to look at it, no matter how many times I told myself that I was a boy from the mean streets of Durban trying to eke out a living in a mean world, I could not help noticing that I was fast descending into another kind of hell. The skeletons that I thought were safely locked away in the catacombs of history were now rattling in my mind.

I sat down to write my story.

# Grandpa

In Soweto they say, *"Wie se laaitie is jy?"* Whose son are you? In Zulu we say, *"Ungowakwabani?"* It means essentially the same thing. There are no easy ways of responding to the question because it arrogantly tells you that you cannot exist in a vacuum. You have to be somebody's son. You are not a statistic, but part of a long human narrative. You don't exist in isolation.

Whose son are you? The question and greeting imbues you with a sense of humanity because it doesn't dismiss you as an abstract entity, but someone who is supposed to have intimate connections with the rest of humanity. *Wie se laaitie is jy?*

Again, the question asks you, subtly, to peel away the many layers of yourself for the pleasure and scrutiny of the inquirer. In a way, it robs you of your individuality, which, as a concept, is still anathema to African society. In African society a child does not belong to a parent only: it (we don't have the pronouns he and she in Zulu) belongs to the community. The modern notion of children who have the right to divorce themselves from their own parents in courts of law is unthinkable. *Wie se laaitie is jy?* At another level, the question offers possibilities of acceptance. Perhaps by opening yourself to the other, you might discover – in fact, there's an inherent hope on the part of the other – that you share the same ancestor. Blood of my blood.

So, when you introduce yourself in African society, you start by saying, "I am so and so, son of so and so, who did such and such to so and so's son, when so and so's son did this and that, under such and such circumstances . . ."

The introduction becomes a narrative that says that you acknowledge and respect where you come from. This tie with the past is inevitable.

In all the years I have known my father, he has introduced himself as Bhanoyi, son of Bhambatha. He is a former peasant with only three years' formal education who was transplanted to the cities where he became part of the working class. Israel Bhanoyi, son of Bhambatha, great-grandson of Mzilikazi, son of Mashobane, son of Khumalo, and so the narrative goes on. The Khumalos are a big and famous clan, part of the Zulu nation. We came to prominence during the height of Shaka's dominion over large parts of southern Africa, when our leader, Mzilikazi, son of Mashobane Khumalo, an erstwhile small-time chieftain, was appointed by King Shaka as one of his generals and advisors. The two worked hard, conquering smaller clans and tribes, fashioning them into the mighty Zulu nation whose influence was to be felt across the continent of Africa over generations and generations to the present. However, when King Shaka and Mzilikazi had a fall-out, Mzilikazi fled – although we Khumalos prefer to say "he retreated strategically" – with a large part of the Khumalo clan to settle in what is today known as Zimbabwe.

In his hegira from some of his own people, Mzilikazi conquered many smaller clans which he incorporated into his burgeoning amaKhumalo clan. To this day, many people with surnames such as Zwane, Dubazana, Mabaso cite Mzilikazi kaMashobane as their great ancestor because they were conquered by him. As a result, a Khumalo man cannot marry women with these surnames. That would be committing incest.

Mzilikazi also founded the Ndebele people in Bulawayo where they are still revered as *amavulandlela* – pathfinders, trailblazers and heroes who stood up to King Shaka. But when Mzilikazi mooted the idea of breaking away from Shaka's dominion there were those elders within the clan who disagreed with him. When he left, they stood their ground and pledged their loyalty to King Shaka. My father's people were among those who stayed behind.

When I was born in 1966, the enchanted past of the Zulu empire was but a distant memory. Indeed, in some people's minds, it was a myth too grand to have been a reality. The pride of place that the Khumalos once held in the affairs of the Zulu nation was history. The very circumstances in which I was born were a far cry from the tales of the aristocratic pedestal which we, the Khumalos, are supposed to have occupied with the blessings of King Shaka.

When I was conceived, my father was working as a stablehand at the horse-breeding and training farm run by the South African Jockeys' Academy, situated just outside Pinetown. My mother was one of a number of women who washed and cooked for the trainee jockeys at this academy. Why my parents were attracted to one another is still a mystery to me. They were poles apart in terms of upbringing, class, religion, levels of education. My mother was an urbanised daughter of a lay preacher with the Methodist church. By the standards of the time, she was highly educated, boasting three years of high school, or what was then called JC – Junior Certificate. She had been born in Cato Manor outside Durban where, before the advent of apartheid in 1948, Africans, coloureds, Indians, whites and Chinese used to live cheek by jowl, unperturbed by race. Upon reaching JC, my mother's parents felt she was educated enough to train for a career in nursing as many black teachers, court clerks, nurses, became leaders in their communities after achieving JC. Very few finished high school or went as far as university. What use was a university education to a black person who, by law, was restricted from some jobs?

Ernest Buthelezi and his wife Beauty – my maternal grandparents – did not have enough money to allow my mother to finish high school, let alone go on to university. Instead they shipped her off to the Mariannhill Mission Hospital where she was to train as a nurse. By this time, Cato Manor, like many "mixed" neighbourhoods, had been demolished. The Indians had been shunted to Chatsworth, the coloureds to Wentworth, the bulk of the blacks to Lamontville, Kwamashu and Umlazi, while some blacks stayed behind in a new township that had risen from the ashes of Cato Manor. The new township was called Chesterville. My mother's family were lucky as they had been allocated a house here, in this place which was emotionally close to their hearts.

It was while she was a trainee nurse that my mother, Maureen Thokozile ("we are overjoyed") Buthelezi, bumped into a dawdling, bumbling country bumpkin who introduced himself as Mandlakayise Israel

17

Khumalo. At a later stage he would point out that he preferred to be called Bhanoyi, "aeroplane". He thought it was a sexy name. It came about partly because as a boy growing up on a white man's farm, he was such a fast runner – he could chase a bushbuck until he grabbed it by the tail and wrestled it to the ground – that they called him Bhanoyi, and the name stuck.

Mama once told me: "Having grown up in the city, exposed to high-flying politicians [Chesterville was the home of ANC leader and Nelson Mandela's contemporary, AWG "Mahlathi Amnyama" Champion] and tsotsis, encountering your dad was a breath of fresh air. I had never seen a person who grew up on the farms. Both my parents had come to the city ages ago. But the minute he opened his mouth, I knew that your father was one of those farm boys. *Inyoni evaleke amehlo* – [a bird which bumbles around with its eyes closed]. His variety of Zulu was slow, with an unfamiliar inflection. I had to listen hard in order to understand him."

Her willingness to listen hard saw the streetwise, fast-talking city girl on her stilettos defeated and humbled by a slow-talking country bumpkin who wouldn't look her in the eye.

There is a picture in the family album which shows two young men posing in a photographic studio. They both look shell-shocked, as if they'd been hauled against their will into the studio. They are standing to attention, their eyes slightly dilated, focusing on the camera.

While their postures are a study in obedience to the camera, or the cameraman, their dress sense is in defiance of the fashion dictates of the time. In many books about that era, black men appear in casual poses, leaning against a post, sitting on the bonnet of a car, resplendent in snazzy Saville Row suits, Stetson hats worn at a rakish angle, a cigarette dangling from the corner of the mouth, and the obligatory two-tone shoes cleaned to a blinding shine. But these two young men wear trousers a size or two too big. They have neckties where their belts are supposed to be. They wear multi-coloured shirts, but of course, because the picture is in black and white, you can't appreciate the Christmas spirit of these shirts.

If you look closely, there is a ghost of a smile on the lips of the young man on the left. That young man is my father. The other young man is his half-brother, David Khefu Khumalo. Asked why they were standing so stiffly, my father told me that the white photographer had ordered them not to move as this would blur the picture. They didn't know what a blur was. They nevertheless obeyed, poor well-trained country niggers who had just fled from a white man's farm in Ixopo, where they were virtual slaves, only to encounter a white man photographer in Durban who bossed them around, and charged them money for their pains.

My father's family had been tenant farm labourers since the beginning of the twentieth century. In the aftermath of the Battle of Rorke's Drift in 1879, large tracts of land, which black people had assumed to be their God-given right, suddenly fell under British rule. In the Ixopo area, the Catholic Church itself appropriated large chunks of land. According to Helen Gamble in her book *Mariannhill: A Century of Prayer and Work*, Sir George Grey, the governor of the British-held territories, ensured that whites amassed as much land as possible. Also, a variety of taxes were imposed upon black people. The British strategy was simple: blacks could only raise cash for their taxes by doing odd jobs for whites. Not only did this ensure that they couldn't attend to their own farms, but, as a psychological ploy, they felt inferior to the whites who employed them.

While preoccupied with the uprisings by the black people in the Eastern Cape earlier in the nineteenth century, Grey had ignored the rising militancy of the Zulu people. He had also forgotten to create foundations for the spread of Christianity and British interests in these parts. He did not take long to remedy the situation. At the behest of the governor, some two hundred Trappist monks from Germany, under the leadership of Abbot Francis Pfanner, settled in Natal along the banks of the Umhlathuzane river near what is today Pinetown. It was here that they established the Mariannhill Mission which still exists.

In the wake of the Rorke's Drift defeat, the Zulu people scattered throughout the province. Many had been rendered homeless. In the chaos of the times, monks from the Mariannhill Mission took away Zulu women from polygamous marriages and accommodated them in a home at the mission. The African had to be rid of his heathen ways, which included praying to his ancestral gods and taking many wives. The African had to be taught that it was his duty to serve the white master. The African had to be taught that he could not own land.

One of Abbot Pfanner's first projects was a printing press which he saw as "the second branch of the pulpit". Soon Mariannhill Mission Press was printing many of the publications of the Catholic Church in South Africa, spreading the influence of Christianity, and thus helping to tame the natives and turn them from their barbarous ways. The church and "western civilisation", and the gun were flipsides of the same coin. Heads, we give you Bibles; tails, we shoot you.

Once the printing press was operating at the Mariannhill Mission, a Zulu newspaper known today as *UmAfrika* ( "the African") was established. (Decades later I would be recruited by this newspaper.) Off this press also came a stream of Bibles in English and Zulu.

The tentacles of the Catholic Church stretched from Mariannhill to many parts of the country, including Ixopo. A mission called Mariathal, which was to play an important role in the lives of later generations of Khumalos, was established around this time.

During the land-grabs at the turn of the century, a militant Zulu figure came to the fore – Bhambatha, son of Mancinza, son of Zondi of the area called uMdlovana, in what is today Greytown. He was an embodiment of a wider discontent. Since the defeat of the Zulus in 1879, which ended black resistance to white rule in the nineteenth century, a variety of disasters seemed to conspire against the black people: a plague of locusts in 1895, rinderpest in 1897, the Anglo-Boer War from 1899 to 1902, and then East Coast Fever swept through the nation. Living standards among traditional black communities deteriorated sharply.

Then, in August 1905, the Natal government passed the Poll Tax Bill aimed at extracting a pound a year from all unmarried black men. This was the final straw. People looked to Dinuzulu, the erstwhile leader and direct descendant of King Cetshwayo who had beaten the British at the Battle of Isandlwana, for leadership. But Dinuzulu acquiesced to the authorities, instructing the people to pay the tax.

Collection of the tax started in January 1906. Bhambatha, who was a minor chief himself, refused to pay. His reasoning went something like this: "Why must I pay the white man tax money for the simple fact that I have cattle? Why should I pay the white man money for the simple fact that I am alive, inhaling God's air, on land bestowed upon me by my ancestors and uMvelinqangi (the one who was here before all of us – or in the white man's language, God)? Why must I pay the white man to continue raping my land?

Where am I going to get the money anyway, since it is the white man who manufactures money? Clearly, the white man wants me to leave my cattle in the pastures, abandon my plantations and go and slave on his land, make his own cattle fatter, draw water for him! The day I do that will be the day when the sun shall fall from the sky to be plucked by my hens."

Emboldened by Bhambatha's resistance, and his promise of violence against the white authorities, thousands of Zulu men joined him in a defiance campaign that became known as the Bhambatha Rebellion and lasted from April to December 1906. At its end, 2 400 rebels had been killed by the military, while 4 700 received jail sentences ranging from six months to two years. Twenty-five of the leaders were deported to the island of St Helena, where King Dinuzulu had been detained before being stripped of his powers and reduced to an ordinary chieftain salaried by the white government.

Although the Bhambatha Rebellion was short-lived, it left a lasting impression in the minds of the peasants who wanted access to land that they regarded as theirs, peasants who still longed for strong leadership and resistance to white rule. The rebellion showed that the people had not lost their fighting spirit.

It was into this troubled time that my grandfather was born in 1907, and the reason his parents decided to call him Bhambatha, a tribute to their hero. It is a comforting thought that during those challenging times my grandfather's parents had the courage to name their off-spring after the white government's enemy number one, Bhambatha.

In 1913, the notorious Land Act was promulgated, further dispos-sessing black people of land. As Sol Plaatje, the pre-eminent writer and one of the founders of the African National Congress, put it, one morning in the year 1913, when the native woke up from his fitful slumber he was shocked to learn that the land he had thought belonged to him had fallen into the possession of the white man. He was now landless in his own land. He either became a tenant labourer on the land which he had been forced to give up, or he was forcibly removed to newly-created settlements.

I can relate to this because one day my grandfather's family at Ixopo had a farm of their own, the following day they learned that that piece of land had been incorporated into a mammoth farm owned by one Mr McDonald whom the Zulus called Madonela. They'd never seen the man before. They were given two choices: either kill all your livestock, or sell it to Madonela. He told them they couldn't graze their cattle on *his* land. So they held a series of feasts, eating their cattle; but they couldn't feast forever, so they sold to the white man. They were left with just two cows for milk.

I learned all these stories from my grandfather. By that time Umkhu-lu was in his fifties and a man about town. He was always immacu-lately dressed, sporting a nicely pressed shirt, braces and a cravat on weekends.

Unlike other old men his age, he never drank traditional beer; he preferred brandy. His conversations were seasoned with English words and phrases. He had the affectations of the *Amazemtiti* – the black peo-ple who were exempted from "native laws"; the urbanised, educated class of black people in Natal who could vote and could drink white man's liquor. Mkhulu's hair, which was greying by now, was always close cropped, and his moustache carefully trimmed. He carried a news-paper under his arm, and would refer to it now and then for news on politics. He was also a great follower of horse racing and boasted to his friends that he had the hottest tips in town. Yet he never won.

Whenever he recounted his hardships on the farm, he would end the story by saying, "And after all the stories I've told you, you're still reluctant to go to school and university? You must have your mind read, my boy. Education is the only weapon you have against the white man now. Learn his wisdom, he will learn to respect you and give you opportunities which the other undeserving blacks certainly won't get."

As he told the story, my grandfather said he was but a boy when his father's farm was taken over by Madonela. He was angry at the sudden turn of events. While he had worked hard and happily under his father's supervision, knowing that the land belonged to the family, when he was forced to work for the benefit of the white man, even at a young age, he began to drag his feet.

Then one night, when he was already in his teens, he ran away from home to seek a new life on the mines of Johannesburg. But the white man's law caught up with him and he was sent back to the farm where Madonela and his own father whipped him. By now the Khumalos had reluctantly begun to accept the ways of the white man. My grandfather and his siblings were baptised in the name of the father, the son and the holy ghost at Mariathal Mission and given western names. Bhambatha was given a new Catholic name, Clement.

When he finally came of age, Bhambatha was allocated a piece of ground on the property where he could build a hut and start his own family. His first daughter was born in 1939, followed by another daughter in 1942. The first son, my father, was born in 1943. By this time my grandfather's father had passed away and my grandfather had to take care of his own family and of his mother.

My father was five years old when my grandfather ran away from home for the second time. The responsibilities to the white farm owner and the rest of the Khumalos now fell on my father's shoulders because he was the only male in the household. Soon he was working on the farm alongside his mother MaMtshali. My grandfather's behaviour epitomised that of black men of his age at the time. The black community was at a crossroads. As Alan Paton noted in the opening pages of *Cry, The Beloved Country,* with nothing to sustain them young black men went to the cities; the villages became the domain of old men and women.

Indeed, the tales in Paton's book are echoes of the stories of courage and deception that were to characterise my relationship with my father from the time I began to talk.

He always used to open his stories with the words, "Your grandfather used to say . . ."

When my father was about ten or eleven, a stranger appeared at the door of the Khumalos' house. The tall gangling man wearing a suit, his crinkly curls parted at the side as was the style of the time, had a nicely trimmed moustache. He had a suitcase and a broad smile. My father should have smiled back for the stranger smiling at him was his own father, a man still in debt to the white masters.

Sometime in the afternoon, inside the rondavel in which the Khumalos had their meals, MaMtshali was on her knees blowing hard at the fire in the hearth in the centre of the room. She had spent a long day in the fields with the other women, hoeing the white man's land so that the weeds wouldn't choke the white man's plantations. My grandfather, who had spent most of his first day at home indoors, was sitting on his stool in the corner designated for the head of the family, sipping home-brewed beer and regaling the children with stories about the big city of Johannesburg.

Then the door flew open. A mountain of a white man rolled in. In his wake were two black men.

"Khumalo," the white man said cheerfully in Zulu while still standing near the entrance. "I see you are back from the city?"

My grandfather was speechless.

"Ah, Khumalo has learned new ways in the city. He doesn't even greet anymore. Nor does he have the decency and the humility to offer other men a sip of his beer. He doesn't even have the courtesy to stand up when the white man comes in." The white man clucked his tongue pityingly, shaking his head. He was smiling. The silence in the room was disturbed by the crackling of burning kindling. Wisps of smoke rose to the soot-blackened rafters. The children were as still as statues, wondering what the white man, whose short temper was well-known, was going to do next.

Then he said, "Khumalo, come and greet the rest of the people who have been missing you all these years, people who have been helping maintain your piccanins while you were living with the ladies in the big city."

The white farmer was the son of the original owner. Grandfather was led to *enkundleni*, where the white farmer normally held court, resolving disputes between the black people on his farm. The *inkundla* was already packed with people who were, like the Khumalos, tenant labourers on the farm. The chattering crowd fell silent at the approach of the white man and my grandfather who was flanked by the two black men as if he were a prisoner.

A long sjambok, a bucket of water and a piece of rope were placed in front of the white man who took off his shirt, showing off his body which had been chiselled into a bronze machine of bone and muscle by years of hard farm work. He began to flog my grandfather.

The sjambok and the rope, or *intambo,* have long been symbols of oppression and conquest. The master used the rope to tie your hands together before he flogged you, while you flinched and flopped about in a futile attempt at blocking the stinging bites of the sjambok.

If he chose, the master would use the rope to tie you to a tree and set his dogs on you. Those passing by would stare helplessly as the dogs tore at your clothes, at your flesh, until you confessed to the theft of the white man's cattle. In some other cases, still being reported in the new millennium, the white master used the rope to tie the culprit to the back of his truck and drag him around the streets.

In particularly severe cases, the aggrieved white boss used the rope to hang offenders. In Zulu, the death sentence (especially by hanging) is simply called *Intambo* – the rope.

# Ubaba

My FATHER – *ubaba* – will never forget that afternoon when his own father was humiliated in front of other people by that white man, who was actually younger than grandfather himself. Many homes – black or white – have a sjambok in the collection of cultural accoutrements, but my father has never owned one.

A year or two after the flogging, *ubaba* ran away from home in search of the glitter of the cities. The tongue-tied, respectful, blundering man must have had a bad time in the city for the city spat him out immediately. He came back home a broken young man. He was fourteen. When the white man tried the whipping treatment upon the boy, grandfather intervened, pointing out that the boy had not tried to run away but had merely gone on a long visit to kwaNokweja in the Ixopo district, where his aunt lived. The aunt had to administer some herbs to him as he was undergoing *ukuthwasa,* in other words the people in the world of the spirits were entering his body, trying to convert him into an *isangoma,* a traditional healer and seer. Grandfather's lie saved my father from the wrath of the white man. But a few months later, my grandfather ran away again. Again the burden of looking after the family fell on the shoulders of *ubaba* who did a brave thing this time. Instead of tolerating the nagging and the insults of Madonela, who fell on the family in the wake of grandpa's latest flight, *ubaba* told the white man that he was relocating the family to another farm.

The family found refuge on a farm owned by the Catholic Church. In exchange for a roof over their heads and land for their crops they had to declare their undying commitment to the Church and Christ. They became devout Catholics, but continued secretly to practise the traditional rituals, such as slaughtering beasts at appropriate times for the appeasement of the ancestors.

Life on the farm was demanding. My father, a good hunter, had less and less time to spend on hunting, and he realised there was a need to earn money. In addition his mother had started hinting that she was tired of washing clothes for an old man like him. She meant it was time for him to find a wife. She already had a *makoti* in mind. Instead my father left for the city. At the age of twenty my father arrived in Pinetown and was told to report at Native Affairs if he wanted to have his pass endorsed with a special permit which gave him the temporary right to look for work in a white town.

"It was inside the Native Affairs offices that I was shocked speechless," he would later remember. "We were made to stand in a queue. Old men, young men, middle-aged men all waiting to have their passes stamped in order to get permission to look for work in the town. The queue was moving slowly. I wondered why. As I neared the head of the queue I realised why. After the white man at the table had had a look at your pass book, he called another white man who was dressed in a white coat to come and 'look' at you."

When my father finally reached the table, the white man behind it snatched his pass book from him and paged through it. He asked him where he was born and checked that his response corresponded with whatever was written in the book. Then the white man in the white coat told him to drop his trousers. When he hesitated, my father had his knuckles rapped with a ruler by the impatient white man in the white coat. Swallowing his pride, he dropped his trousers in front of all the men in the hall. Then the white man in the white coat started probing his penis and testicles with a stick.

"Okay, boy, you can go. Don't go sleep with the *skebereshes* [bitches] of Durban. They will give you VD. Hear, boy?"

"Yes, baas." My father was a good nigger who knew his place in relation to the white man. The probing with the stick, he was to learn later, was supposed to be a medical examination to ensure that the black man was not bringing venereal disease into white South Africa. Those with a swelling or some sores around their privates were dispatched back 'home'. Outside the hallowed confines of the Native Affairs offices, black men never spoke about their experiences at the Pipi Office as it was called. Black people could joke about anything including death, but they couldn't joke about what happened inside the Pipi Office. My father was obviously angry at this dehumanisation. He blamed the African National Congress and the Pan Africanist Congress for offending the white man and goading him to such an extent that he decided to devise these new stringent laws to keep the blacks away from his cities.

My father accepted a job at the stables run by the Jockeys' Academy without even asking what his salary was going to be. He simply wanted to work and save money so he could pay *ilobolo* for a *makoti* and start his own family.

As my father and his country bumpkin friends reasoned, "Why fight the white man? Why bite the hand that feeds you?"

"Who wants to end up like that fool Nelson Mandela, languishing in some island jail for trying to challenge the white government?"

"The white man is old in his wisdom. The black man had better accept that his gods have turned their backs on him. He must bow before the god of the white man."

The news of my father's romance with a city girl called Thokozile travelled fast, and by the time it reached Ixopo it had been embellished to say that the lovely Bhanoyi had already started paying *ilobolo* to the family of this city girl.

"Do they observe our *ilobolo* rites these people of the cities?"

"These city people are confused. They are straddling two worlds, trying to live like white people – except that they are not accepted in the white world – while also observing some of our Zulu rituals."

"And our poor Bhanoyi has joined their ranks. He's beginning to talk the white man's language as well."

My father's problems reached a climax when it turned out that my mother was pregnant. I was doomed before I was born: a child of a bumbling country bumpkin and an equally bumbling city girl who was dumb enough to be impregnated by a country bumpkin in the first place, putting paid to her prospects of ever going back to Mariannhill Mission Hospital to complete her training as a nurse. The Catholic hospital frowned upon trainee nurses who bore children out of wedlock.

# Umama

WHENEVER I AM ASKED ABOUT MY ORIGINS, I always respond: "I was born in Chesterville, Durban."

But this is not entirely true. In fact, it's a lie. When I was born my parents were living in the stable-hand quarters at the Jockeys' Academy, but I was delivered at Mariannhill Mission Hospital. The reason I give Chesterville as my place of birth is because this is the township from which my mother – *umama* – came. This was also where her parents and her other siblings lived when I was born. I also choose Chesterville as my place of origin because it's a township with a history of toughness. Chesterville was the bedrock of Durban politics where the AWG Champions of the African National Congress plied their trade; where gangsters such as Boy Qhogola flashed their blades; it was, too, the birthplace of the renowned journalist Nat Nakasa.

To be precise I was conceived in the servants' quarters at the Jockeys' Academy in a tiny room within close proximity of the stink of horseshit and the constant neighing of the gentle animals. And the moment I was born I lived in defiance of the laws of apartheid which dictated that the likes of me had to be sent to the rural villages where we rightly belonged. By being born in a white area, living on a white property, I was growing up against the laws of the land. Yet my mother had to resist my father's desire to send me to my grandparents in Ixopo. And even at a tender age, the idea of Ixopo didn't appeal to me.

Ixopo was a distant mythical village lovingly conjured up by my father in the stories he told when nostalgia got the better of him. His stories were teeming with trees, buck running wild, rabbits, men using sticks to settle old scores, rivers gurgling, birds singing at the brightness of the flowers, children sitting around huge bonfires listening to old women telling stories about the enchanted past when Zulus were still kings. But these were just myths. My mother's stories I could relate to. They spoke about fast cars, about hoodlums wielding knives, about colourful clothes.

They say that when I was young, I loved to recite lines which no one had ever heard before, that I liked to sing songs which existed only in my own world. One of the songs which my mother still recites, which she swears was composed by me as a toddler goes something like:

> *Ingulube encane, yay'endalini, yakuqeda ukudla kwayo,*
> *ayisayiboni indlela eya ekhaya*
> (the small pig went to the auction, and quickly finished his food,
> but then he couldn't find his way home . . .)

My given name is Vusisizwe, "the one who is going to revive the nation". How noble, how naïve, how optimistic. How parents always foist upon their children names alluding to challenges they themselves had failed in their youth. *The one who is going to revive the nation.* How unfair. When I had to be baptised, the officiating Catholic priest gave me the name Frederick, an anglicisation of the German name Friedrich, the ruler of peace. Imagine that? *The ruler of peace!* Because I was fat, my mother gave me the nickname Marlon, after her favourite film star, the chunky Marlon Brando.

During working hours, I was always at my mother's side as she went about her chores in the academy's huge kitchen. Even when Bongani, my baby brother, was born and strapped to her back, crying and dribbling, doing everything he could to steal the limelight at my expense, I would spend most of the day with her. Although now and then I used to slip out to play. An old white woman who seemed to be the owner of the academy – a woman the black labourers called Gogozi – had a couple of children almost my age who stayed with her. They were probably her grandchildren.

I used to play with them despite the language barrier because children don't need words that much. You just play. Kick ball, throw stones at birds, chase after each other, play swing, eat as much as you can, fart and laugh. Who needs words in such a world?

One day my white friends simply disappeared. I had no one to play with. I cried. My mother told me to keep quiet. She told me that the white children had gone to a faraway place called boarding school. I was left to invent my own solitary games, some of which turned out to be dangerous.

It is said that I've always been inquisitive. But my parents never thought that my curiosity would one day almost lead to my death.

Something colourful or shiny must have induced me to crawl underneath a car parked in the academy's yard. When the driver drove off, I was still underneath, fiddling with the pipes, holding onto the engine casing.

My recollection is vague, but the car dragged me about a hundred metres before an alarmed passer-by saw me and alerted the driver who stopped the car. They had to pry me out. But it was the alarmed voices of the adults that made me to cry, not the bruises I'd sustained while being dragged or the fact that my shorts had been torn off.

And then one bright summer afternoon my white friends came back for the school holidays. They spoiled me with gifts of toys and sweets. We played and played. We gesticulated, threw our heads back in laughter. I learned some English phrases. But mostly we played and laughed without using words. We adored one another, my white friends and I. It was around this time that one of the elder children gave me my first horse ride. But in the evening the white kids went to the main house, while I went to the back room where my family ate, relaxed, slept. Our meals were leftovers from the white trainee jockeys at the main building, where, at any given time, there could be between thirty and fifty apprentices. (One of them was Michael 'Muis' Roberts who was to become an international jockeying legend.) As jockeys are trained to watch their weight we were never short of food. And good food at that. Sausages, steaks, vegetables, puddings, the lot.

If anything darkened these days it was my father's talk of taking me

TOUCH MY BLOOD

to Ixopo when I was ready to start school. I would break down in tears. The stories he'd told me about boys fighting with sticks, chasing after buck, milking cows filled me with horror and disgust. Why would I want to chase after some poor buck, or look after cattle in some god-forsaken forest when there was so much good food to be eaten at the Jockeys' Academy? The good white man had done the job of slaughtering the beasts for us. All we had to do was cook and eat. Thankfully, my mother, too, was opposed to the idea of my being posted to the farms. She was protecting her interests too. She'd never seen the inside of a rural hut herself, let alone crawled on all fours smearing a piece of ground with fresh cow dung, pretending it was floor polish.

"When we get home, I will teach you how to milk the cows. And the women will teach your mama how to collect water from the river and fetch wood from the forest," my father would say. "I will build you a big house where you and your brother will have your own room, your own privacy. This life we live here, sleeping in the same room with children, is not good."

He would further boast that he had been sending money 'home' to his stepmother. By that time granny MaMtshali had passed on and grandpa had taken a new wife, MaKhuboni. The money he had sent 'home', he would add, had been used to buy more cattle for the kraal.

My mother would see red. "I'm not going to a rural village. If you want to marry me, you will find me a house in one of the townships. Kwamashu, Umlazi, Chesterville. There are so many townships springing up all over the place. Rural life is dying. City life is the future. Children must go to school instead of wasting their time looking after cattle which are being killed by successive droughts anyway."

Although she respected my father, my mother had a mind of her own thanks to her liberal upbringing in the townships where children were listened to. Her parents, both of whom were relatively well educated, had instilled in my mother a sense of pride and independence. Which is why I occasionally wonder what attracted her to my father.

My mother was a city girl, used a hot iron comb to straighten her hair, smeared her lips with red rouge, and scrubbed the blackness out of her face with skin-lightening creams. Apparently she even tried to remove one of her front teeth, in keeping with the fashion of the times, but my grandmother, thank God, prevailed upon her not to do that. In as much as my mother was fun loving and in touch with the fashions, she never smoked nor drank; my father's vice was smoking, even dagga. But the weed didn't agree with his constitution and he would become wild, picking a fight with everyone he met.

I was five years old when my parents married. By then they had three children. The ceremony took place in Dassenhoek, a semi-urban village not far from Pinetown. All I recall is that it was held at the house of one of my mother's cousins. After the ceremony, and recognising his increasing familial responsibilities, my father confronted his employers. He said, listen, my family has grown bigger and I want to move out of your premises and find my own shelter. He said, listen, these children must go to school in the not too distant future. He said, listen, this is 1971, the beginning of a new decade and I am a new man. He said, listen, I need a salary increase.

This man who previously had been unable to look a woman in the eye when he spoke to her, who had used a necktie as a belt, who had criticised both Nelson Mandela and Chief Albert Luthuli for "provoking the white man and causing unnecessary trouble" had become a forceful, citified man who knew his rights and who was seen by many of the workers at the academy as a leader.

His employers refused to increase his salary. My father resigned in anger. But by resigning he had to vacate the room. After some negotiations the bosses stipulated that my father, my brother and I had to vacate the premises, but my mother was given a few months' grace while she nursed their baby daughter.

My brother and I were carted off to Chesterville to stay with my maternal grandparents. My father shifted from pillar to post but was banned from the premises of the Jockeys' Academy for being insolent enough to ask for a raise.

My maternal grandparents, the Buthelezis, had a brood of grandchildren under their care. The children's mothers – my aunts – worked in distant cities where they lived with boyfriends who did not want to share their lodgings with children. It was easy to dump the children with the grandparents and send some form of stipend to the old couple at the end of the month. My brother and I were yet another addition to this convocation of piccanins running about the over-crowded four-roomed hovel that the long-suffering couple called home.

One of the bedrooms was occupied by my aunt and her husband. The other was occupied by my grandparents and a couple of grandchildren. The rest of us had to sleep in the living room and the kitchen and the passage. I slept with two of my cousins under the kitchen table on pieces of cardboard. We covered ourselves with two flimsy blankets. Much was different for me here. Whereas in the past I had eaten from my own plate, here I had to eat from a huge bowl with a brood of greedy bullies who sometimes spat into the food simply to put you off, so they could enjoy the food in solitary splendour.

Whenever you complained to grandfather he would simply grunt, "Why don't you punch them out of the way?" and continue chomping on a chicken leg while we children had to be content with dollops of porridge floating in an insipid, lukewarm liquid masquerading as chicken soup.

*Umkhulu* Buthelezi, as we called our grandfather, wasn't a mean man. It's just that there wasn't enough money and food. He promised us that if we went to school and worked hard, we would in our later lives have enough money to have meat with every meal. Each of us would have a whole chicken to himself. Imagine that! Because I was one of the youngest and also the least experienced in these endless wars over food, I almost always went to bed on an empty stomach.

But as time went by I learned the tricks. *Umkhulu* Buthelezi would tell us to kneel and close our eyes while he said grace. When everybody had their eyes closed, I sank my hand into the bowl of food. The word "amen" was an indication that the troops could descend on the bowl. By that time I had extracted my first fistful of porridge. There would be pushing and cursing as the fastest of the children plunged mucus-stained hands into the bowl. There was no time to chew. You just had to shovel the food into your mouth and swallow, hoping you wouldn't choke. By the time they swallowed their first mouthful I would be going for my third, snivelling my mucus and sweating from the pressure of coarse porridge on my small gullet.

The menu was predictable: thick slices of brown bread and tepid water masquerading as tea in the morning. Ditto lunchtime. Supper varied from stiff porridge and boiled cabbage leaves to stiff porridge with boiled ox blood which the grandparents bought from a local butchery, to stiff porridge with boiled potatoes flavoured with curry powder. At the end of the month, when our mothers had sent money, the food would improve. Instead of ox blood, we had to fight over a mound of chicken feet which my grandmother boiled and flavoured with coarse salt. Sometimes it would be chicken heads, other times it would be ox tripe. During my stay there I never tasted real meat. Rice and pudding were things to dream of.

My twin cousins were much older than me and always took the lion's share at mealtimes. They were big fellows and I couldn't pick a fight with them. I don't think it ever crossed their minds that this mousy boy from the white people's kitchen prayed that they should be knocked over by a car and die. I hated them for bullying us and eating all the food. But I still couldn't fight them. Eventually I started bullying the twin's youngest brother who was my age. The twins didn't interfere. However, when that primordial instinct of brotherhood took them, the twins held fast my hands while their young brother was allowed to punch me to his heart's content. The other boys in the family kept a safe distance whenever I was turned into a punching bag.

In the streets, my cousins were never on my side. They invited strangers to bully me. They knew my past, for whenever I wanted to show my superiority I bragged that I had been raised in a white neighbourhood, eaten white people's food, played with white children, worn clothes which smelt of white people. Indeed, I occasionally found strands of white people's hair in my clothing!

"Yeah, you doubting black monkeys. What is this? What is this, huh! Can't you see this is a strand of a white person's hair?"

"Come on, this is no white person's hair. This is dog hair."

"Listen to the monkey who's never seen a white person. A monkey who's never smelt a white person. This is white person's hair, you monkey face."

The group converged on me to consider the evidence. Yes, they nodded sagely, this was a strand of a white person's hair.

Emboldened by this confirmation, I cried out triumphantly, "Yes, you thought I was lying! The shirt I am wearing used to belong to a white boy. Yes, smell it! Don't be jealous! Smell it! You see, I told you. This is a white person's smell. Not your stale urine black-monkey smell. This is clean white-person smell. Told you, told you. I know white people as I know myself, promise you. Can even speak their language. Yes, I guess you've never seen a white person's shit."

"What does it look like, and smell like?"

"Not as brown and tough as a black person's shit. It's kind of yellowish, soft. From the good food they eat."

"But it still smells," one of the boys said, wrinkling his nose.

"Of course. But you have never seen a naked white body. I mean, a white woman walking naked, I'm telling you."

"Listen to him now telling another lie. Listen to him. Listen to the black white boy. Listen to the black boy who thinks he's white. Listen to him!"

"'Strue's God," I cried. "Cross my heart and hope that I die, I've seen white people naked. Jumping into a swimming pool in the nude. I guess you've never seen a swimming pool in your life. I'm not talking about that smelly puddle with frogs in it where you swim."

That attracted an avalanche of punches from the boys who evidently had been hoping all along that I was going to insult them, giving them an excuse to vent their jealous rage on me.

"Oh, let's see if your white people are going to come and protect you now. Where are they?"

"Guess you've never seen a real black dick," one of them said, spraying me with a jet of urine.

Oh, how I missed my white food and my white friends and my white games where there were no punches and kicks. I wondered what would happen if you punched a white person in the face. Did they bleed like us? I thought hard, trying to remember if I'd seen a white person bleeding. No, I hadn't. At that moment I wished a white boy could appear so I could punch him hard on the nose. Just to see if he would bleed.

After beating me up, the boys cleaned my bleeding nose under a tap. They warned me not to tell on them. That night I didn't share jokes with any of my cousins. After all, they had not helped me while I was being beaten up. In fact the younger brother had participated in the attack on his own blood. I sullenly prepared our bedding under the table and immediately went to sleep.

I was lying on my bedding and a big rat was smiling at me, its teeth exposed. Its eyes full of humour. Its whiskers twitched as it crawled towards me. It showed its pink tongue, started licking my face. I cried out, "No, don't do that!" – bumping my head against the table as I tried to get up. I had been dreaming. But there was a commotion in the kitchen. Everybody was up on their feet, towering above me, children crying. Above the din I heard the voice, "You are lying, *madala*. You are hiding some illegal people in this house."

"No, *nkosana*, I am telling you God's honest truth. These are all my grandchildren. Their parents are working in the cities. The only adult people in this house are my wife here and myself."

The accusers were three policemen dressed in black uniforms. They were municipal policemen – blackjacks – whose job it was to make sure that everybody in the township had all the necessary papers and a passbook with all the required stamps and endorsements.

"Okay, let's see your passes now. Yours and your wife's."

My grandfather shuffled to his bedroom. My grandmother tried to comfort the younger children who were still crying. My grandfather came back and handed over their passes. These were carefully inspected then returned.

"These children are not supposed to be here. The white man's law says they must be sent back to the farms, to the homelands where they belong."

"But they were all born here in the city, all of them, and so were all my children . . ."

"Don't argue with me, *madala*." The policeman, who could have been my father's age, prodded my grandpa with his nightstick.

Tears rolled down my grandfather's cheeks.

"The next time I come here, all these noisy piccanins should have disappeared. The white man is trying to clean the city, and your children are busy breeding, dumping their urchins in this township. We want Chesterville to be a model city. We want to win the mayor's medal for order and good citizenship and people like you want to deny us the opportunity. Get rid of these children from this township the minute I turn my back on this urine-smelling hovel of yours, do you hear?"

My grandfather whimpered something. The policemen disappeared into the night. For the first time I had witnessed the brutality of an oppressed black person towards his own kind. When my grandmother broke down in tears the whole houseful of children wailed until my grandfather produced his belt and shouted at us to shut up. Afterwards grandpa told us to kneel and pray to the Lord for the rude policeman's forgiveness. His faith in the Lord was legendary. Not only did he make us say our prayers before we went to sleep every night, he also compelled us to go to church every Sunday, something I wasn't used to. He was a strong believer in the goodness and kindness of the Lord. God helps those who help themselves he would say, adding the inevitable rider that the first step towards helping oneself was to go to school, acquire the white man's education. There was no use challenging the white man if you were uneducated, fumbling about in darkness.

That night, while my grandpa droned on about how the proud shall be humbled on judgement day and how the meek would inherit the earth, I was wishing my eldest cousin and my uncle had been present when the rude policemen came to the house. They would have torn the cowardly policemen to shreds. Such a pity they were in jail for doing exactly what they were good at – breaking into white people's homes and stabbing people. They were in and out of jail, those two men.

When they were out, they enjoyed telling us about their jail experiences. "Don't ever go to jail," they would advise. "Things are bad inside there."

Then my cousin would teach us how to box, how to protect ourselves in the street. And our uncle, who had lost all his front teeth during a fight in jail, would shake his head at our amateur boxing efforts and say, "You think the enemy is going to allow you the luxury to show off those fancy left jabs and right hooks and what have you? The enemy will just do this" – and he would produce a huge knife and start stabbing the air furiously.

"Now, can you beat that?" he would say triumphantly, flashing us his smile, squeezing his tongue into the gap between his teeth. "The knife is still the best. No fancy boxing shit. Give me my knife any time." Then he would show each one of us how to handle the knife properly. There were delicate steps you had to follow if you wanted to scare the enemy a bit or cut him lightly with the blade. There were also moves for maximum impact if what you wanted was to bring the enemy down. My uncle's advice was learn how to use the knife, and *use* it if necessary. Or learn how to run away fast.

The two men were in jail when our soccer side, Chesterville United Brothers, hosted Ndunduma Home Boys, a club from Clermont, a settlement north of Chesterville. Clermont had a reputation as the home of tough guys. All the big "clevers" – the bank robbers, the dice throwers, the numbers people, the muggers, the killers – hailed from the sprawling, undulating hills of Clermont. Not that Chesterville didn't have its fair supply of thugs, but, by its sheer size, Clermont could easily decimate us if war ever broke out between the two settlements. So, when we learnt that one of the biggest sides from Clermont was coming to play us, the news was received with mixed feelings by the adults. Some old people were happy that the soccer team from our small humble township was going to silence the loudmouths from up north. Others were worried that the violence that was sure to explode at the soccer stadium would create such animosity between the two townships that it would take generations for the anger to subside. No one wanted to make enemies of the people from Clermont.

39

On the day of the game the boys from Clermont arrived with a fan-fare. We watched from a hill near the soccer stadium as a cavalcade of cars – Cadillacs, Valiant Regals, Dodge Monacos – snaked along the main street to whistles of admiration. Once they had parked their cars the men strolled down the street, puffing at their cigarettes. They were resplendent in their Viyella shirts, Pringle cardigans, Stetson caps, Florsheim shoes. Soon a group congregated at one of the stands and the unmistakable aroma of dagga permeated the air.

The teams started prancing about on the field, flexing their muscles. A black cat ran across the ground to loud cries of outrage. Cats have always been associated with witchcraft, and could be used to trans-port *umuthi*, bad medicine to bewitch your enemy.

The referee blew his whistle and the game started. About three min-utes later the boys from Clermont scored. We soon equalised. Clermont scored again. This was to be their last goal because somebody in the stands started a fight. Pangas were produced, forests of sticks mate-rialised and all hell broke loose. Even the players were attacked. We ran for our lives as people threw bottles and bricks. The visitors ran for their cars and screeched away while their pursuers rained stones on them.

One of my uncles was in town that weekend and I saw him chop at a few heads with his panga.

Because Chesterville was such a small township, the impact of the fighting at the soccer grounds touched all the residents. The injured ran into neighbouring houses dripping blood and there was general confusion. When the screams of outrage, the cries of anguish and the excited shouts of victory died down, a silence settled over the township. The violence was over. For now. Yet late that night we heard windows being broken, car tyres screeching, people screaming. For the first time I heard gunfire. In those days guns were scarce. We realised then that the boys from Clermont couldn't allow their reputation as tough guys to be tarnished by a small township like Chesterville.

It was very late before tranquillity finally returned.

The following day, people milled about the streets, talking excitedly. There were shards of glass everywhere, trails of blood. People, swathed in bandages, stopped cars in the streets, asking to be rushed to various places. The twins led us on a tour of the streets to inspect the damage, one of the boys giving a running commentary on the fighting. Near the soccer grounds a pack of dogs fought over a corpse. As we approached they ran away and, for a moment, we stood there frozen by the sight. One of the twins bent down and removed the dead man's watch, saying he would sell it. The rest of us threatened to tell on him but he pocketed the watch as we all ran home.

We breathlessly told the story to grandfather. He was angry, but my cousin didn't come home until late that night and the following day avoided my grandfather.

News of what had happened in Chesterville reached my mother and it wasn't long before she had us transferred to her cousin in Dassenhoek. We stayed there for a few months before moving into our own new home, a four-roomed house in a new township called Mpumalanga outside the industrial town of Hammarsdale.

Despite the problems and the overcrowding at my grandparents' place, I was sad to leave Chesterville. Over the years, I have been back to sit with the twins under our favourite avocado tree, reminiscing about our childhood, talking sadly about that fateful soccer match. There is a song composed by someone who was there and saw people chopped by pangas.

It goes:

*"Ngo-1971, eChesterville,*
*kwasuka isidumo ngomfanyana,*
*owakhuluma kakhulu, kwacasuka abadala.*
*Igama lakhe nguThule . . ."*
(In 1971, in Chesterville,
hell broke loose over a boy who spoke too much,
offending the elders. His name was Thule . . .)

I often wonder what happened to Thule, whoever he was, whatever he said to spark such an orgy of violence.

# Mpumalanga

When saints are ceasing to be saints
When devils are running back to Hell
It's the Moment of Rise or Crawl
When this place becomes Mpumalanga
With the sun refusing to rise
When we fear our blackness
When we shun our anger . . .
MAFIKA GWALA, "No More Lullabies"

MPUMALANGA – "a place where the sun rises", in other words, the east –
conjures up images of a tranquil, sun-kissed haven where people smile
with joy and contentment at the bountifulness and fecundity of life.
Indeed, when we first arrived in Mpumalanga, there was a palpable
sense of joy in the air. Everything about the township – the neat rows
of four-roomed brick houses, the tarred roads – was new. Even the sand
that blew in the windy streets seemed new. People walked around
smiling, heads held high, chests sticking out, brimming with the joy
and pride of being new owners of new houses in a new township. The
houses were the same in shape and size, but painted in a variety of
pastel colours.

Our pink house stood at the corner of the street with the number
C576 neatly printed above the main door. The streets were clean, not
a piece of paper billowing around, not a dog turd to foul the air. I saw
trucks sprinkling something granular on the pavements and in people's
yards which were still bare and sandy. These granules turned out to be
seeds of a new strain of grass supplied to all homeowners courtesy of
the benevolent people from the municipality. Within days grass sprouted all over the place. Soon the township would be green and liveable.
There would be less dust. There would be birds twittering about in the
wattle trees which also seemed to have sprouted in our yards almost
overnight.

After my father and some of his friends had off-loaded our pieces of furniture and other domestic paraphernalia from the van we'd hired, my father led us into our house. By our standards it was big – two bedrooms, a kitchen, a dining room-cum-lounge and a toilet. That my brother and I had a bed to ourselves, a whole room to ourselves, catapulted me to cloud nine. No more overcrowding and discomfort.

The house itself was simple: the walls bare with exposed bricks, the floors cement. There was no ceiling, the asbestos roofing clearly visible. There was no kitchen sink. In the bathroom there was a toilet and a shower. No sink or bath. But who was complaining? This was not the white man's Jockeys' Academy where they had a big bathtub and warm water. In fact there was no electricity then; we used candles for light and paraffin for cooking. But there were streetlights which bathed the township in their blue glow at night. This was a black township after all, in a country run by a white government. We had to be grateful to the government of the KwaZulu homeland which had received funds from the white government in Pretoria to build this sunny township.

The distance from Mpumalanga to Chesterville was about forty kilometres, but by moving here we had, by law, renounced our South African citizenship. The territory within which our township fell was another "country" called KwaZulu.

So here we were, proud Zulus who had been designated their own place under the sun, not to be bothered by whites, or other tribes. However, although we were on our way to self-rule as a tribe, in order to be gainfully employed we had to cross over to the factories in "white" South Africa. As it happened, the nearest industrial area to our township was Hammarsdale, two kilometres away with a booming textile industry. Our township was a reservoir in which the white factory owners of Hammarsdale fished for cheap labour. But we were not complaining. At least not for now. There were jobs in the factories so people wouldn't starve. There were the new houses for those who were gainfully employed. The only recurring complaint from older people was that they were not legally allowed to keep animals for slaughter. Whenever they needed to slaughter an animal to observe a specific ritual they had to buy a beast from one of the white farmers on the periphery of the township.

By the end of the first week, we had settled into our new home and were enjoying every minute of it. It was spacious, mostly because we did not have much furniture. In my mother's bedroom was a three-quarter bed, a wardrobe, a dressing table, all hand-me-downs from her employers. In our bedroom was a single bed and a suitcase packed with toys and comic books. These were also courtesy of my mother's white employers. In the kitchen stood a table, two chairs and a bench. We cooked on a Primus stove that sat on the floor in a corner. In another corner was a basin where we washed the dishes. My father's favourite chair took pride of place in its own corner.

As I've said, our house was on a street corner. Life had us cornered.

Our groceries – sugar, maize meal, flour, one or two onions, three or four tomatoes, a bottle of cooking oil, a packet of salt – were stored under the table. In the lounge-cum-dining room were two sofas and a coffee table, also from my mother's employers.

"Loyalty has its own rewards." My mother would swell like a peacock as she pranced about her house. "I have served these white people loyally for all these years, and I am being rewarded now. Look at my furniture. No woman in this neighbourhood has such beautiful furniture."

In that she was right, many of our neighbours' houses were still devoid of furniture. But it wasn't a big neighbourhood as the township was still under construction. We were among the first lucky ones to move in.

My mother still worked at the Jockeys' Academy, which had since moved to a village called eNtshongweni, or Shongweni as white people persistently, but erroneously, called it. This meant she had to commute by bus. My father did odd jobs for a construction company and a shopkeeper in Pinetown, an hour's bus ride away. For some reason there were a few months when my parents were unable to live at home so my maternal grandmother came to look after us. Even after my parents had solved their commuting problems she stayed on, despite my father's complaints that she was one more mouth to feed.

My brother and I didn't mind because granny was fun to have around. Not only could she cook up a storm, she also had thousands of stories and fairy tales to tell. These stories flowed with amazing eloquence especially after she had had some home-brewed traditional beer which she bought from our neighbours, the Hadebes. Because granny had been born and brought up in Pretoria, she could speak Sotho fluently, to the great pleasure of the Hadebes.

When my grandmother was tipsy she sometimes used to say in front of my father: "I wonder what my lovely daughter Thokozile saw in this uneducated cowdung-smelling moegoe!" (Because she was urbanised, she not only spoke Sotho, Zulu and English, but also Afrikaans and tsotsitaal.)

Legless from the beer, she would sway in the middle of the kitchen where the family was gathered around the Primus stove, and talk to herself.

One day she teased my father about his accent, which truly sounded strange to we urbanised Zulus. When she realised that my father was getting agitated, she said, "Ag, shame, sorry *mkhwenyana* [husband of my daughter]. I don't mean to offend you. But you know what, I like my country bumpkin *mkhwenyana* because he loves his children. I seriously think my Thokozile made a right decision by choosing a blind bird from the sticks rather than going for a streetwise thug from the city who would pump her stomach up . . ." she moved her pelvis, ". . . and leave her miserable."

I suppressed my laughter. Then my grandma laughed out loud, making faces at my father.

One day my grandma started with the teasing as usual, but my mother snapped and slapped her hard. The old lady, her legs already weak from the booze, flopped to the floor, laughing hysterically. Then my father jumped from his chair and slapped my mother who screamed back at him. I started crying. My brother started crying, and my grandmother cried because she realised she had caused all the trouble.

My brother and I were sad when, a few weeks later, our granny went back to Chesterville.

But before she left, my father taught my mother to teach her mother how to brew traditional beer. It was a funny process. When my grandmother wanted to brew her own beer, she approached my father for advice about ingredients. My father, always the demure boy from the sticks, couldn't speak directly to his mother-in-law so he would relay his advice through my mother.

In the end my grandmother was grateful to my father for the tips, for beer is a symbol of goodwill, it is a sign of hospitality, it celebrates the gathering and giving of news.

# Chickens for Africa

THERE'S A SAYING that you can take a darkie out of the bush, but you can't take the bush out of the darkie. There is an element of truth in this. Witness my father. He had been in the city for many years but deep in his heart he was still a country boy. No sooner had we moved into our house than he built a huge makeshift shelter and filled it with chickens. He was good at breeding them, and soon started a brisk trade in the squawking, clucking, cackling creatures. Chickens, like goats, are an important part of life. Whenever you had to communicate with the ancestors, you had to spill blood. If you couldn't afford a goat, you had to use a chicken. My father was always ready to sell one for these important occasions. Of course people also bought the chickens for the pot on payday.

Once I carelessly forgot to fasten the gate of the fowl run properly. Soon the chickens were all over the yard, jumping through the wire fence and buzzing about the street. They invaded our neighbours' vegetable patches and decimated the greenery. It took my friends and me a long time to catch them and lock them back in the enclosure. My father gave me the severest punishment I'd ever received, flogging me with a long thick branch until my buttocks were sliced open, oozing blood. His was an addictive personality: once he started doing something, he didn't want to stop. If you tried to intervene, he might turn on you. My mother knew this, but she couldn't stand by and watch me being killed by my father. She intervened. And paid a price for it. My father clouted her in the face. But he soon calmed down, muttering to himself, "Eish! Women and children!" Then went out for one of his long walks.

After that incident I had great respect for those chickens. I made sure they were fed and that the gate to their enclosure was locked properly.

The chicken enterprise went a long way towards providing money for the purchase of things we needed in the house. For instance, a coal stove, a brand new Welcome Dover bought from Town Talk furnishers. As soon as it was delivered, the stove took pride of place in the corner that previously had been occupied by our Primus stove. From now on, the house was warm and comfortable during the cold winter months.

On Saturdays mother would wake early, clean the house, do the washing, get the fire going in the coal stove. By the time we woke the whole house would be redolent with the sweet aroma of vanilla essence, flour, cinnamon. Mama would be sweating over the stove, baking sweet cakes and bread.

Mother taught me, as the eldest, how to make a coal fire in the stove, and how to prepare porridge for my siblings in her absence.

Shortly after the arrival of the stove my father bought us a dog. He named it Shaluza Max after his favourite guitarist. The yellow mongrel was good at guarding the fowl run against thieves who had taken to breaking into people's houses while they were away in town working. The secret to ensuring that your dog was alert and always ready to attack intruders was to put generous dollops of hot chillies into his food. This process of enraging your dog was called *ukuxhaphisa*. After all, you didn't want a dog that was friendly to strangers. You wanted a dog that not only barked at anything that moved, but pounced on everything that moved.

As he was also a man with green fingers, my father established a large vegetable garden which, in summer, would flourish with spinach, carrots, pumpkins, sweet potatoes, onions, tomatoes, beetroot and, of course, maize. Neighbours took to buying vegetables from us.

When it was not planting season, weekends were lonely. As we didn't have many neighbours there was no reason for us to go out. We stayed indoors, playing with our toys or paging through our comic books. It was during this time that I developed a love for books. Even though I couldn't read, I followed the stories by looking at the pictures. Kid Colt chasing the Red Indians. Roy of the Rovers showing his soccer prowess. And so on. I loved the characters as it was easy to lose myself in their fantasy world. At any time I could be Zabata cracking the skulls of the bad guys with intricate karate chops. I could be the gun-slinging Kid Colt blasting away the Apache Indians with his Colt 45. Often on these weekends my father, who was himself bored and evidently had nothing to do as he didn't have friends in the township, decided to while the time away by trying, once again, to rouse my interest in things that he had left behind in his village of Ixopo.

One of these activities was Zulu stick fighting. Initially, I hated it. He would give me two sticks and take me through the paces. Sometimes we became characters in a movie and passers-by would gawk as father and son engaged in mock stick fighting, groaning or shouting triumphantly. It was embarrassing. Sometimes people made derisive remarks, calling us *amaqaba*, "the uncivilised ones". Nonetheless, the stick fighting skills would later come in handy when the going got tough in the township.

Although the house next door was empty, the one next to it was occupied by the Mkhwanazis. The Mkhwanazis were to remain family friends for a long time, in fact, I look on the Mkhwanazi boys as my own brothers. The stepfather of the Mkhwanazi boys was Mr Dubazane, who became a close friend of my father's. The boys' grandmother was a wonderful old lady who looked after us while my parents were working. She prepared us old-fashioned meals – *isthwalaphishi, izinkobe, isijingi*. She also brewed us *amahewu*, a thick nourishing beverage made of sorghum. And she would regale us with Zulu conquest stories and accounts of how the white men stole the land from her people and burnt the fields and killed the cattle. The stories were told without a trace of rancour; I don't think she realised she was making a political statement. She was just telling tales based on fact and nostalgia for an enchanted past.

The other family in our neighbourhood were the Hadebes in the house just below ours. Now these were colourful people.

The Hadebes were originally from Harrismith. Like many black people they had come to the cities and the surrounding areas in search of that proverbial pot of gold. They believed that it lay somewhere in the factories of Hammarsdale where the matriarch had found a job at a textile factory. The eldest of the Hadebe children, a young man, worked at the Hammarsdale processing plant of Rainbow Chickens. The other boy, about five years older than me, was in my class at school. And not making progress at all.

The Hadebes were good neighbours – at least from a child's point of view. We didn't quite understand their language, but that didn't bother us as they accepted us into their yard to play with the children. The Hadebe yard was always a hive of activity. Basotho men groaning under the heavy weight of blankets which they draped over their shoulders would sit around drinking traditional beer, throwing dice, playing cards, telling jokes, or dancing to the music played on an organ that stood in their lounge-cum-dining room. They could party from Friday to Sunday night with the booze flowing and food aplenty. They lived for the moment, tomorrow would take care of itself. My parents were not rabidly tribalistic or chauvinistic, but they tried to discourage us from mixing with "those baSotho children". They were fighting a losing battle because we enjoyed the cheerfulness and the food. It was at the Hadebes, for instance, that I learned to differentiate edible rats from vermin. After my father had harvested his maize in the summer, the field would suddenly be infested with huge brown rats that had yellow stripes on their backs. They were called *izimbiba*. The Hadebe boys taught us how to trap these rats which I had never noticed before. At close quarters these creatures were beautiful, cuddly. And once you'd skinned them, gutted them and roasted them on an open flame, they were a finger-licking delicacy. Thanks to the Hadebes, my culinary horizons were widened.

The Hadebes were the first family to boast a *gumba-gumba*, a large music system that played LP records. Soon after they made this glamorous purchase other families followed suit. Our section of the township became a loud vibrant haven where people sauntered down the street with a sprightly musical spring to their gait. You could hear the wailing organ of Jimmy Smith, the soothing sounds of The Staples, the rousing lyrics of Curtis Mayfield, the haunting guitar of Philip Tabane

50

and Malombo, the groovy *mbaqanga* beat of the Soul Brothers, the understated soulful observations of Mpharanyana Hadebe, the socially conscious, deeply felt cries of Marvin Gaye.

The Hadebes were also the first to open a shebeen in their lounge. They offered an array of beverages from clear beer – Castle lager and Lion ale – to illegal concoctions. Men came from different parts of the township to relieve themselves of the stress of work and loneliness, and to be relieved of their hard-earned cash. Once their appetites had been sharpened by the booze, they bought boiled pig trotters or roasted sheep's heads. I had never seen people eating sheep's heads before, but after eating a morsel of sheep's ear, I decided that I had been living in foolish ignorance of this wonderful food.

It was also in the Hadebe yard that many of us learned to pick pockets and throw dice. Here, too, we witnessed bloody knife fights. People would spill each other's blood with knives and pangas, then sit down and break bread, drink beer and laugh together even before the blood had dried on the ground.

It was also at the Hadebes that I learned how to doctor drinks so that people would be knocked out while apprentice pickpockets practised their skills. Initially, pinches of snuff were enough to knock out a victim. But later, the Hadebes and many other shebeen owners put drops of car battery acid in the sorghum beer during the brewing. Battery acid was so dangerous that sometimes, instead of sliding into unconsciousness, the victim would become wild, banging his head against the wall, biting himself. On two occasions I saw men howling with delirium tremens. I thanked God my father wasn't a drinker.

While the Hadebes already had a brood of children, their house was a transit camp for those from the rural areas of the Orange Free State in search of work and a new life.

Mrs Hadebe was a charming lady who had a succession of male admirers. She was generous in both spirit and body. All her nine children had different fathers. The eldest daughter, Sdudla, who was in her late teens or early twenties, had taken after her mother in the art of winning and breaking the hearts of men. In a weekend she could devour four men and go on to dance her feet off, gyrating to the pumping music of the organ. Her reservoirs of energy and charm were bottomless. We knew about her sexual escapades because we used to sneak up on her while she and her lovers were sweating it out behind a bush.

"God gave you your body and you owe it to yourself to not only enjoy it, but also give others joy," she would shout nonchalantly when she was drunk, to the dismay, shock and horror of our parents. "There's no use being stingy with your body because at the end of the day the ants and the maggots will eat it. That's for sure. *Dlala ngento onayo!*" Play with what you have! The Hadebes gave meaning to this famous line by the poet Mafika Gwala:

> And you once asked why blacks live so fast
> love so fast
> drink so fast
> die so fast . . .

Sdudla wasn't beautiful in the conventional, physical sense. She had internal beauty. She had charm, a glow that stirred one's emotions. Even at that age I was moved by her. Her young breasts were pear-shaped and seemed to fight against the imprisoning confines of her bra. Like their owner, who sometimes felt imprisoned by societal norms, her breasts wanted to break free. Her face was round, her eyes smiled involuntarily. Her complexion was cocoa-coloured.

One weekend, one of her boyfriends caught her in the arms of another man. He was so angry, so distraught that he tried to commit suicide by locking himself inside his car and setting it alight. He was rescued from the inferno by men who then beat him up for his stupidity. Sdudla shrugged off the incident. Above everything, however, Sdudla had ambitions and thought music would be her escape route from poverty and her passport to fame and fortune. She joined one of the local bands as a singer-dancer. And because she was a jovial outgoing person, she was popular with both band members and fans. In a way, she was successful. But real success in those days was measured by the number and size of cities you had worked in. Sdudla headed for the bright lights of Johannesburg. There, we heard, she rubbed shoulders with famous music producers and could be seen at the popular night-clubs. Then one night a jealous lover plunged a knife into her, killing her.

Our other neighbours, the Malefanes, were not much fun. Although they too were Sothos they avoided the Hadebes. The mother was a teacher at a distant town called Hillcrest, the father a manager at a company in Pinetown. Until then I had never heard of a black person being a manager of anything. Yet Mr Malefane drove a VW Kombi and his wife drove a Fiat. Until then I had never seen a black woman driving a car. Nor had I seen a boy my age wearing spectacles as did one of the Malefanes. Surely things like these were not supposed to happen? The Malefanes were strange people. The boys wore shoes every day of the week and not only for church on Sunday. They wore under-pants like the white kids at the Jockeys' Academy. They tried to play with us, to learn our language, but their mother was too protective. Almost every five minutes she would call out from the gate, "Aaron, Joseph, *tlokwana!*" which we soon learnt meant "come home!" When the mood took her, their mother spoke to them in English.

"Aaron, Joseph, supper is ready!" "Aaron, Joseph, your lunch is get-ting cold!" To the rest of us, food was food. There was no distinction between the meals because it was bread and tea in the morning, bread and tea during the day, although, if we were lucky, there might be por-ridge and cabbage at night.

My friend Thilo joked that my parents had no need to cook meat or stew anymore. If we sat outside the Malefanes with our plates of por-ridge while they were eating what they called supper, the meaty smells coming from their house would be enough to help us eat our thick por-ridge with relish and pleasure.

"They are having sausages," Thilo would say, sniffing the air hun-grily. "Lovely, juicy sausage." Or: "Aaron's mother put too much chilli in the stew today. It's too spicy and it's making me sneeze." And he would sneeze repeatedly.

Thilo was not a close friend but he was to have a lasting impact on my life. He was fond of fighting. Whenever he saw two boys fighting, he would find a reason to join in. Yet he wasn't a good fighter. Because he was light in complexion, he bruised easily. A punch to his nose would let loose a stream of blood. But he would not cry and run away. He would resort to the trusted method of a hopeless fighter: find stones and broken bottles with which to attack his adversaries. Thilo was also naughty, forever leading us on raids into people's fruit trees.

One day we raided the yard of Mr Mfene, a foul-mouthed man who greeted passers-by with a "Good morning, your mother's private parts, did you make your wife happy last night?"

At first people were offended by Mfene's utterances, but then came to make fun of his surname which, in Zulu, means baboon. Mfene, however, was a Pondo, a small tribe famous for their foul language and excellence in witchcraft.

When he realised that somebody had trampled over his patch of vegetables in a bid to reach his peach trees, Mfene made it known to all and sundry that he, a true-blooded Pondo, would bewitch the thieves. That he had an ugly face marred by long, thin tribal scars and only one eye, cast him in the role of a wizard, at least to our young minds. Why hadn't we realised this before we offended him, we asked ourselves?

Without waiting for more threats, Thilo led us to Mfene's yard. We found him sitting in front of his kitchen leisurely eating a boiled chicken with his hands.

"You are the thieving boys, huh?" he said after Thilo had explained our mission.

"*Yebo, mkhulu,*" we chorused, "and we are sorry for it."

"Why didn't you come and ask *mkhulu* for permission to pick the peaches? You know *mkhulu* lives by himself and can't finish all the peaches."

"Sorry, *mkhulu,* we won't do it again."

He smiled and told us to go. Then called us back, saying, "Have some meat with me."

We hesitated. We couldn't possibly eat a wizard's chicken. Our parents had warned us not to eat from the plates of strangers. We mumbled our apologies, except Thilo who readily accepted a piece of chicken. We soon followed suit.

In the years to come, Mfene would slaughter a whole goat and eat it by himself, bragging, "You Zulus are so poor you have to share a goat among a hundred people. Look at this Pondo here, he is enjoying a goat by himself."

Mfene had a succession of women who lived with him briefly before leaving in tears, hurling insults at him. We heard our parents whispering that he was obsessed with divorce. If divorce was a reference to the stream of women visiting a man one after the other, most of us believed divorce was something that should be tried by men who love the good things in life.

# Bewitched

"All kaffir boys eat mealie-meal and do not
think at all" – A SCHOOL RECITATION

IN 1973 I STARTED SCHOOL at the local Ubhedu Primary School. It was
not to be a good year.

The first disaster was an epidemic that afflicted chickens. The chickens in our yard, about a hundred of them, were not immune. They soon
developed sores around the eyes, their feet swelled and they lost feath-
ers. They also stopped laying eggs, from which we had made a steady
income. They didn't eat, they couldn't walk. My father, who had nursed
ailing horses back to health and was good with herbs, set about saving
the ailing chickens. He prepared concoctions that were a mixture of the
gooey aloe juice, manganese potassium and warm water. With pains-
taking care he forced the mixture down the throats of each chicken.
Within days some of them began to recover. They ate the grain, and
laid eggs again.

But the revival didn't last long. The chickens began dying one after
the other. Our yard was rank with the fetid stench of chicken illness,
the mephitis of death. Flies were everywhere.

My father was devastated. The sale of chickens had provided us with
necessary cash. Within weeks the whole fowl run was decimated. We
went back to eating porridge and vegetables, and meat became a rarity
once again. The little money that my parents made went towards the
repayments on our stove and other pieces of furniture.

The second disaster, at least from my point of view, was the birth of
my second brother. His arrival meant that my sister, who had been
sleeping in my parents' bedroom, now moved into our bedroom to share
our bed. We were getting crowded and I didn't like that one bit.

The third disaster was that my father had developed a zealous love
of soccer and become involved in the launch of a local soccer club. To

start the club money was needed to buy the kit, balls, boots. In addition, there were transportation costs, and some sort of reward was required for the players' efforts. The result? My father and his partner had to dig deep into their pockets. That did not bode well for us. Our welfare was being compromised, bread being snatched from our very mouths.

Suddenly our house became a hive of activity with youngsters walking in and out of our home. The kids who were lured to join the Silver Stars were a mixed salad of characters: some were juveniles of unremitting delinquency who had spent time at reformatories; others were from broken families and needed a father figure (a role that my father played reluctantly and at the expense of his own children); others simply had no respect for older people. They smoked cigarettes and dagga in front of my father until he lost his temper and caned them. Fridays were the worst. The players had to "do camp" at our house, in other words, they slept overnight so that they would stay away from the pleasures of the flesh, waking up physically and psychologically ready for the Saturday soccer match. My father now lived for the soccer team.

"These soccer rascals of yours are stealing food from the mouths of my own children," my mother complained.

"This is the beginning of great things," my father would retort. "Kaizer Motaung and Jomo Sono are where they are today because they started small like us. Somebody had to make sacrifices for them to succeed. Please be patient. This club here is going to produce great players. And we will all be rich and successful."

"I am talking about now. Now! My children are starving. These things of yours are bringing scabies to this house. They are bringing all manner of disease. They are bringing foul language. They are sniffing benzine. Our children will pick up the bad habits from these gutter creatures of yours."

"What do you want me to do? Leave talent to rot in the township's gutters? You want me to tell these poor kids to go to hell? There's one thing you forget. Were it not for the kindness of other people before

57

me, I wouldn't be here in the city. I would still be somewhere on a white man's farm. Someone had to give me an opportunity to come here and eke out a living. It is therefore my responsibility as a good Christian and civilised person to do likewise for all these youngsters. They have a future ahead of them. I have to help them, guide them."

"Yes, but not at the expense of my own kids, our own kids!"

"Eish! Women are trouble," my father would suddenly say, walking out of the debate, "Eish!"

If a soccer match were to be played on Sunday, my brother and I would be in trouble. Mother insisted that we go to church with her; father expected us to help carry the soccer paraphernalia to the stadium. He expected us to share his passion for the game, to study all the important moves so we could improve our game. Unfortunately, we couldn't be at both places simultaneously. To avoid shouting matches between himself and my mother, my father devised a strategy. If a Silver Stars game fell on a Sunday, we would attend the early church service, then sprint back home to help him.

My father's plan eased the tensions somewhat, but my mother continued expressing dismay and anger at the "waste of my children's money". Relatives and friends of the family were surprised that my father, always a loving father and a considerate husband, had suddenly become a wild soccer-crazy person who behaved as if he had no family to worry about. There were dark rumours and whispers that my father had succumbed to the bad medicine of neighbours who were jealous of the peace within our home. In a word, my father was bewitched.

While my father's soccer fever was at its height, I volunteered as a trainee altar boy. My parents were surprisingly encouraging for I had thought my father would be angry as I would be spending more time in church than at the soccer stadium.

Instead my new status triggered something in him. One night, he called me to sit next to him and spoke in a language I couldn't understand. He looked at me expectantly. "You are supposed to respond. I am the priest and you are the altar boy."

My mother intervened, "It just goes to show how long ago you've forsaken your God, how long you've been away from the church. Mass is no longer conducted in the Latin, it's said in Zulu."

"Jesu, Maria, Josefa!" my father cried out in horror. "How can you speak to angels in Zulu?"

My mother and I laughed, but my father was truly flabbergasted. Reluctantly, he began to accept the reality and helped me with my catechism. Later he enlisted the help of our devout Catholic neighbours in my training. The neighbours were an elderly couple who lived by themselves, quietly devoted to each other and to the Lord. Their home was a study in placidity. No cats, no dogs, no children.. And they rarely spoke. They sat on their chairs in front of their house, staring into the distance. They usually dressed in the brown flowing robes of the Holy Order of St Francis. They were characters straight from the Bible. Except that they were black. Biblical characters were all white, with the exception of a few lost black souls like Simon who picked up Jesus' cross when the Son of God collapsed from exhaustion. Black people have always been willing to carry the white man's burden.

Meanwhile our financial situation got so bad that my mother had to supplement her salary. She bought fresh hake from the supermarket, cut it into pieces which she fried in a thick batter. We were then dispatched to sell these morsels at the soccer stadium and in the neighbourhood. Because I was the eldest and good with numbers, I was responsible for sales. Neighbours called me *umfana kafishi* – fishboy. With the fish business thriving, my mother added boiled eggs to the fare. They proved equally popular. The profits went towards buying schoolbooks, my school uniform, groceries, whatever was needed. But my father repeatedly raided the coffers to prop up his financially challenged soccer team, and the fish and egg business died.

As if the problems at home were not enough, an uncle joined our household while he searched for work. Soon my Uncle Henry turned our dining room-cum-lounge into his sleeping quarters, causing my mother to throw tantrums when he brought "aunties" to sleep over. Her major complaint was that Uncle Henry had a different "auntie" every weekend. Anarchy had been loosed in the Khumalo house.

Even though Uncle Henry ate a lot, enjoyed *ugologo obomvu* (brandy), I appreciated him because he took a keen interest in my progress as a budding soccer player. He had a huge collection of soccer magazines, both local and foreign – *African Soccer Mirror, Sharpshoot Soccer* among them – which he had amassed over the years. It was through these magazines that I learned of the South American players such as Pele and Jaihzinho (who was later to play for Kaizer Chiefs), and of Platini of France, Kevin Keegan of England, Eusebio formerly of Mozambique and later Portugal.

Because he could read a bit of English, Uncle Henry translated the articles for my friends and me and taught us the rules. Not only was he well-grounded in soccer theory and history, he was also an industrious trainer and player for Silver Stars. He instituted a routine of jogging ten kilometres two afternoons a week, and sometimes my father joined us. His problem, however, was that he couldn't pace himself. He would sprint like a harassed springbok for the first three hundred metres, only to drop out and go home to drink copious volumes of water and lie on his stomach on the lawn. My uncle was surprised that even at eleven years old I could keep pace with the rest of the team.

Thursday was reserved for "ball work". This meant practising how to shoot at goal, how to tackle, how to keep goal, and the general improvement of our ball-handling skills.

It was during these sessions that my uncle's sharp eye identified our skills.

During practice I was allowed to experiment with various positions – from goalkeeping, to defending, to striking. I preferred goalkeeping. This for a number of reasons. My hero was the famous goalkeeper and my namesake Frederick "The Cat" Mfeka. But more particularly I realised that if your defence line was strong, as goalkeeper you could spend a large part of the match watching the rest of the team running and sweating. If the ball happened to come your way you could always entertain the crowds by engaging in amazing acrobatic moves – spinning in the air or diving for the ball – especially if the shot was tired and slow. Goalkeeping was also fun because if someone scored against you, you could always blame it on your defenders. "You let the enemy past! Not only that, when I was right in position to pounce on the ball, you obscured my view!"

On one occasion our junior team was pitted against the Highlanders junior team at the local dusty grounds. Right from the onset I was kept on my toes. After dribbling past our defence line, a left-footed boy called "Masterpieces" Mbanjwa came running towards the goal, towards me. I jumped about in anticipation, my bare feet suddenly hot. (Although we respected National Professional Soccer League regulations we couldn't observe the rule relating to the wearing of boots because many of us couldn't afford them.)

Masterpieces made as if to shoot. I dived to my right. He kicked left. I spun in mid-air and stopped his ball. The roar of the applause was heartening. Frederick "The Cat" Mfeka eat your heart out!

A few minutes later, Sandile "Chain Puller" Mkhwanazi, my neighbour, scored. But after that goal it was clear that we were on borrowed time. The Highlanders became rougher in their tackles, desperate to equalise at all costs. My defence line was under pressure. I was on my toes, my heart throbbing with excitement: I could not allow a goal after the exquisite save I'd made.

A big-headed Highlanders boy called Rhee who, although he couldn't run fast, could dribble the whole defence line including the goalkeeper, took possession of the ball around the centreline. Steadily, skilfully, he dribbled his way towards me.

Above the throb of my heart I could hear the noise as if of angry bees of "Rheeeeeeee" resounding around the spectator stands.

"You fools, stop that man!" I cried, pointing at my comrades who kept falling on the ground as if pushed by a malevolent god. "Put him down! You, Doom, get up from the ground and tackle that man!"

Rhee was coming my way. I jumped about in anticipation. When he entered the penalty area, I started towards him. Rhee did the unexpected. In mid-stride, he fired a shot at me. I leapt in the right direction, but I had miscalculated. The ball hit me smack in the face. I was out for the count.

I came to a few minutes later with people towering over me, voices crying out, "Ah, he's opening his eyes!"

My father said, "Eish! That's a relief. Can you take him back to keep goal again. He was doing quite well."

My uncle said, no, the boy needed a rest. Common sense prevailed.

I was soaking wet and bloody. Because I had lost consciousness I had been doused with water to bring me round. After that I was done with goalkeeping. Frederick "The Cat" Mfeka could keep his crown. Instead I became a defender.

There is a poetic, philosophical poignancy to my encounter with the boy they called Rhee. A few years later we would be great friends working together at my Aunt Selina's butchery. But in later years, we would be sworn enemies politically. He became a feared vigilante and hired killer, and helped identify to his comrades my parents' home. He also advised his comrades on how best to ambush me.

But that was the future, now there were other concerns and one of them was my youngest brother, Thabo. From birth Thabo was trained by my father to use his left hand. My father badly needed a left-wing striker and he saw Thabo eventually filling this position. Indeed, the boy who had been born a right-hander grew up to become a hot left-wing striker who nearly became professional – if only school, further study and a diversion into crime hadn't interfered with my father's intentions.

Thabo was about five years old when our Aunt Theresa contracted tuberculosis. She was admitted to Springfield hospital, operated on, and spent four months there recuperating. In the interim she lost her job in Durban North where she worked as a domestic servant. Losing her job meant she also lost the roof over her head. She turned to us. The house was overcrowded, and bedtime was sheer misery. I longed for the days when I had been the only child, sleeping peacefully in my own bed.

Because Auntie Theresa was still recovering from TB, she ate the best food in the house – boiled chicken with vegetables, peanuts, fresh fruit, yoghurt and other delicacies. We children fought for the leftovers.

My mother used to smack us for this because, she said, we would pick up the TB infection. We continued raiding the leftovers, even if it meant salvaging them from the rubbish bin. Such good food couldn't go to waste.

A few months later Thabo took ill. He vomited blood and lost weight. At night we couldn't sleep because of his incessant coughing and anguished cries. Eventually he was taken to hospital and diagnosed with TB. In those days TB could kill. The family was shattered. About five months after his admission to Botha's Hill tuberculosis hospital, I visited him with my father. I'd imagined the hospital as a clean place with women in white running around feeding you the best and healthiest food available. But this hospital was in a village and the grounds were a profusion of weeds and tall grass. When we arrived a boy with unkempt hair and a sling of mucus snaking from a nostril broke away from a group playing in the yard and looked at us with interest.

It was Thabo. He had lost so much weight that his cheeks were hollow and his bloodshot eyes protruded from their sockets. His lips were dry and cracked. His face was so scarred that I had to ask him what had happened.

"We were fighting, uncle," he replied.

"I am not your uncle, I am your brother. Why do you fight?"

"The other boys tried to take my food, uncle."

"I said I am not your uncle. I am your brother. Remember me, your big brother Vusi? Anyway, why didn't you tell the nurses about your food being taken away from you by the other boys?"

"The nurses just laugh at you and tell you to fight for your food."

There was a forlorn look in his eyes, a vacant stare that touched my heart. I felt tears in my eyes and looked away.

Then Thabo said cheerfully, "No one can beat me. I am the best fighter around here. They can only stab me. They can't fight me fist for fist. I can defend myself."

My father stood there, listening to the boy, mumbling, "Eish! The dogs. Eish! The dogs." After the visiting hour we left Thabo wailing, "*Ngifuna umama!* I want mummy. I want to go home."

He still hadn't recovered, so we had to leave him behind to the mercy of those bullies and heartless nurses. When he finally came out of hospital, Thabo had changed. He was violent, insolent and unwilling to listen. That hospital was like a reformatory. Although it cured the young patients, they were moulded into violent boys. Thabo was never to be the same again.

\* \* \*

In first grade my class teacher was a Mistress Khumalo. She hated me even though we shared the same surname. The class was big, about eighty children, most of whom were six or seven years old, although some were already teenagers.

One of the first recitations we learned was in English, a language new and strange to us. Without understanding the meaning we repeated the sounds which Mistress Khumalo drummed into our heads: *All kaffir boys eat mealie-meal and do not think at all.*

I was absent-mindedly reciting these lines at home one afternoon when my mother angrily asked where I had learned these words. I told her.

"Never again should I hear you saying such words," she said, and then explained to me that the words were bad, an insult.

A few weeks later, Mistress Khumalo ordered us to recite the words again. I recalled my mother's exhortation and kept my mouth shut. Mistress Khumalo rounded on me. "You, Khumalo boy! Why aren't you reciting like the rest of us?"

"Mistress . . ." I gulped, sweat breaking out on my face, "my mother said the words were not good, that they were an insult."

"What does your mother know about education? Isn't she just one of the uneducated *amaqaba* from the bundus. Is this her school? I ask you, is this her school? As long as you are in my class, you are going to do as I command! Do you hear? Now, are you going to recite like the rest of us? One, two, three, start . . ."

I didn't take the cue. "Why is your mouth still shut? Do you want my cane to visit your hand, or are you going to recite now?"

"Yes, mistress, I mean no, mistress . . . I can't recite . . ."

Whack! Whack! Two strong lashes landed on my shoulder.

"Recite!"

Tears brimming, I shook my head, no, mistress, I can't.

"Show me your hand!"

I extended my hand so that she could cane me on the palm. Which she did until I bled. Yet I refused to cry. I was my father's boy, stern and stubborn. I bit my lip hard and held back the tears. When she was finished, I picked up my slate and smashed it on the floor, swearing the obscenities I had learned from the Hadebes. Then I ran home, bawling all the way.

My mother was mad. She skipped work the following day and angrily stormed into the office of the principal, Madam Phewa, who listened attentively. The upshot was that Mistress Khumalo was summarily dismissed. But my reputation as a short-tempered, squeaky-voiced boy with a formidable arsenal of obscenities became legendary among the teachers. To ameliorate my bad reputation, I always came first in class. The teachers loved me for that.

At about the age of eight or nine I fell seriously ill and was bedridden. Partly to allow me undisturbed nights, and partly because my parents feared my siblings might contract the illness, I was given a foam mattress and again enjoyed the luxury of sleeping alone. Not that I noticed. I was too sick, not eating, losing weight, and constantly bathed in sweat. Occasionally my mother took time off to nurse me.

What scared everybody most were my screams as feverish nightmares assailed me. To this day those visions loom large and menacing in my mind. They came in various forms. One reminded me of the blood-spattered corpse lying in the street after the soccer match in Chesterville. It would rise from the ground, its head that of a dog, and walk towards me in long purposeful strides.

In another vision I am walking down a street where I encounter a man riding on the back of a baboon which is galloping towards me, grunting, its mouth foaming, its sharp teeth bared.

A third nightmare has me stumble upon a crowd of men dressed in animal skins and colourful beads who chase after me, their gleaming spears poised.

When I recounted these visions to my parents, who relayed them to friends, neighbours and relatives, most people believed I had been bewitched by neighbours who were jealous of my impressive progress at school. These jealous neighbours wanted me to go mad so that I would quit school. Something had to be done.

"What exactly?" my mother wanted to know.

"Go see a witchdoctor who can exorcise your son, get rid of the bad medicine that has been driven into his head by the bad neighbours," came the response.

My mother was a pragmatic Christian and had no truck with witchcraft. She felt I was in the clutches of a common fever which caused "minor hallucinations". Laxatives would sort the matter out. My father took a different view. A man who believed in herbs and the existence of *utokoloshe*, my father insisted that we needed to consult an *inyanga*.

A week later we visited a man by the name of Mkhwanazi at his house in Georgedale, a settlement on the periphery of our township. He had a combination of talents as he practised both as a seer relying on Christian prayer and as an *inyanga* communicating with God through his ancestors. He also used herbs and other concoctions. Mkhwanazi confirmed that jealous people had bewitched me. He prayed over me and gave me some sticky substance to lick. Initially I refused to open my mouth, screaming and bawling, fighting off whoever tried to touch me. But being weak from the illness, I was quickly subdued and the bitter substance forced down my throat.

A day later I showed signs of recovery. I ate again, and walked tentatively about the yard. The visions had stopped.

I have long wondered what sparked those visions. As a child I had been told that bad medicine people, *abathakathi*, witches, rode on the backs of baboons as they went about their nefarious engagements. Perhaps I internalised this image, letting it ferment in my subconscious until the fever brought it out. I've given up analysing these things, but it never ceases to amaze me that poor people always blame bad luck or illness on witchcraft.

A week after our consultation with the *inyanga* Mkhwanazi, I was ill again. Father decided enough was enough. He said he was taking me to his home village of Ixopo where I would be given proper Zulu medicine and divination at the hands of people who knew what they were doing, "not these city charlatans".

I was asleep for most of the three-hour bus journey but arrived irritable and tired, having vomited frequently. Granny MaKhuboni prepared a bed for me and I plunged into a deep, peaceful sleep.

The following day I was woken by a strange sound. I felt better and rested, and quickly got dressed. Outside my Uncle Gilbert sat on a stool milking a cow. It bellowed as he gently squeezed the swollen udders, the milk squirting in thin jets into a bucket. I had never seen a cow at such close quarters. The white people at the Jockeys' Academy had kept a couple of cows for milk, but I had never ventured near them.

"You want to try your hand, little Vusi?" he asked me.

I washed my hands in a bucket of water and joined him. The udders were rubbery and tender and my fingers seemed to tingle as I gently pulled at them. It was a wonderful experience.

Afterwards Uncle Gilbert took me for a short walk, waxing lyrical about the simplicity and beauty of country living. But I still wasn't interested. The houses were rondavels made of mud with thatch roofs and fresh cow dung smeared on the floors. People cooked on an open fire in the centre of the rondavel. If you were thirsty you drank lukewarm water with things floating in it, water that had been fetched two or three days earlier from the river some three kilometres away. These people had nothing in common with us township folk – except, perhaps, poverty and suffering.

They spoke a slightly different dialect of Zulu in a tone so sluggish you almost fell asleep. Their lives were even more circumscribed, narrower, shallower than those of black people in the cities. Their levels of ignorance gave me an opportunity to shine. I seemed very knowledgeable and educated as I told them stories about the "civilised" food we ate in the cities, that we lived in houses that had taps inside, that we slept in beds while they slept on grass mats, that our toilets were inside our houses and could be flushed. I had to explain what a flush toilet was because these people who visited the bush to respond to a call of nature, if they didn't have pit latrines in their yards, couldn't imagine it. While I was there I preferred to use the bush rather than squat in the smelly latrines. Even so, wiping was a challenge. These people had not yet discovered the conveniences of toilet paper. They used any kind of paper. But then, paper was a luxury, as I soon discovered, and old newspapers were reserved for the use of adults. Boys my age showed me how to use tree leaves. The more innovative used stones. Others would slide down a grassy knoll as a fun playful way of wiping.

Late in the afternoon, my father and uncle took me to the *inyanga*. As we walked down the meandering paths my father would pause now and then to marvel at the undulating hills covered in a thick blanket of green. Cattle grazed in the distance. Women and children worked on their smallholdings. Men, sweating in the heat, repaired fences or mended their roofs. The air was alive with birdsong.

My father said one day he would like to come back and live here, closer to nature, establish himself as a farmer on this land.

"Live here?" I asked incredulously.

"Yes, then you will learn to be a real man, to respect our Zulu traditions."

My uncle interrupted – and I wanted to hug him – reminding my father that it wasn't worth coming back "home" anymore, that the green land, the rolling, fecund hills that he was admiring actually belonged to a white farmer. That blacks were confined to the other side of the green hills, to the red hills, the broken hills whose skin bled when the rains fell. The dead land where plants did not grow. Even though some people like my father were fooled into believing that their land had been returned through the homeland system, it was clear to me that the hand of the white man was everywhere.

Finally, we arrived at the house of the *inyanga*. By rural standards this was a mansion: a cluster of about thirteen rondavels neatly arranged in a crescent. At the centre was a huge courtyard and inside this a small kraal where the calves were kept at night. Parked nearby were a tractor and a bakkie. This was clearly the house of a rich person. The yard was redolent with the sweet-sour smell of cow dung. After shouting our greetings from the gate, we were let in by a boy and escorted to one of the rondavels.

The *inyanga* did not live up to my expectations. He did not fit the Rider Haggard stereotype of a man in animal skins, his face covered in ochre, his eyes bloodshot and demonic. Nor did he bellow like an injured bull, spitting at invisible adversaries. True, the walls of his "consultation room" were draped in a variety of animal skins and dried herbs. But the man himself was dressed in jeans, running shoes and a T-shirt. He greeted us warmly, calling us by our clan name, amaNtungwa, and welcomed us to his "humble" place. He knew that my father was knowledgeable about horse racing and betting and asked for some tips.

Eventually the *inyanga* knelt, mumbling while he gazed intently at the rafters. He dug into a skin bag, drawing out a fistful of divination bones.

He repeated, in slightly different words, what had been said by *inyanga* Mkhwanazi, that I was bewitched by people jealous of my progress. To counter this he further prescribed that once we got back to our township home we should slaughter a goat to appease the ancestors and pray to them for protection. He gave my father a bag of herbs to be boiled and administered to me whenever I became feverish. He then burnt a handful of dried leaves, forcing me to inhale the smoke which stung my eyes and made me sneeze. End of consultation.

For supper that night Granny MaKhuboni served two broilers and steam bread. We feasted, washing down the mouthfuls with sour milk which she drew from a big gourd. This surely was good, tasty, nourishing food. Afterwards we sat supine around the fire while Granny, my father and my uncle regaled us with stories, but as the night wore on, the stories inevitably degenerated to witchcraft. Because I had spent a long time listening to my mother's teachings, I remained sceptical.

For instance, during the summer storms lightning occasionally killed people. But many refused to acknowledge that lightning was a natural phenomenon. They believed that witches used herbs and incantations to kindle bolts of lightning to dispatch those they had grudges against. And people suspected of being witches would be attacked and stoned to death, or had long sharpened sticks driven up their anuses, *ukujoja*. I sat beside the fire listening to the stories, but I could tell fact from fiction, unlike my cousins.

The next day it was time to go home. I had fully recovered from my "demons," as my father would have it, or from my fever, as my mother preferred.

# Fever

NOW A FEVER OF A DIFFERENT NATURE took root in the township. The victims were, well, most of the residents. The person who bewitched them was a man called Chief Mangosuthu Gatsha Buthelezi. People adored him. People swooned at the mention of his name.

"*Somlandela somlandela uShenge, somlandela yonke indawo. Somlandela somlandela uShenge; lapho eya khona somlandela,*" – we will follow him, we will follow Shenge (Buthelezi's clan name), we will follow him wherever he goes, they sang, corrupting an old hymn – "we will follow Jesus, we will follow him wherever he goes . . ."

Buthelezi, the leader and founder of Inkatha yeNkululeko yeSizwe, was the new messiah destined to free black people, especially the Zulus, from white bondage. The first step towards liberation, according to the agitators in favour of Buthelezi, was the full independence of the Kwa-Zulu homeland, where Zulus could govern themselves without the interference of the white man.

As the Buthelezi fever gained heat, teachers were made to sign pledges of loyalty to the man and the movement. Those wishing to run businesses needed Inkatha membership cards to apply for premises and trading licences.

Suddenly everything revolved around Inkatha: at school children were taught "*Ubuntu/Botho*" – or good citizenship. As a concept *Ubuntu* is a commendable foundation for nurturing good behaviour, good neighbourliness, good citizenship. The worrisome factor was that Inkatha's activities centred around the leader.

When Buthelezi visited our township early in 1976 most residents flocked to the stadium to listen to the "messiah of the black people". He appealed to people to resist terrorist propaganda. He said children should respect their parents, their teachers and their councillors. He said there were bad winds blowing towards our townships, winds inspired

71

by the communists and the terrorists who were bent on turning the country into a bloodbath.

We should fight against our white oppressors and regain our dignity, yes, but we should conduct our fight peacefully through non-violence. He said we shouldn't play into the hands of the communists who intended taking over the world. He said Inkatha was taking a vanguard role in fighting for the liberation of the black people.

Buthelezi was a knowledgeable and highly educated man, we were told. A graduate of the University of Fort Hare, where the likes of Nelson Mandela, Oliver Tambo and Robert Mugabe had also studied. In addition, Buthelezi was also a man of many talents: a good orator and a competent movie actor appearing in a number of movies including the epic *Zulu* about the rise and fall of the Zulu empire.

Waving our flags of green, black and gold – colours that Inkatha had usurped from the African National Congress – we sang with Buthelezi:

*"Ayanqikaza ayesaba amagwala, athi kungcono sibuyele emuva;*
*qiniselani nani maqhawe; sekuseduze lapho siya khona . . ."*
(the cowards are doubting, shivering and scared, they say it's better we turn back; stand firm oh ye brave heroes; we are getting closer to our destination . . .)

Inkatha fever swept through the province as we were cajoled into an allegiance with Buthelezi and his Inkatha. Disagreement was tantamount to denying your Zuluness.

Gradually the administration of our schools and of the townships was transferred from Pretoria to Ulundi. Rebellious teachers opposed to the homeland vision were fired and labelled terrorists.

Terrorists became the manifestation of evil. The South African Broadcasting Corporation devoted regular programmes called *Isenanelo sezindaba* to analysing the word *amaphekulazikhuni* – terrorists.

Terrorists were those people who killed peace-loving black people; terrorists were used by the communists who wanted to take *our* country away from us. Ironically, in these discussions of terrorism black people were granted the privilege of being South African again, and not mere citizens of the homelands. People were promised lots of money to help the police apprehend terrorists. Nor was it difficult to spot these terrorists. They spoke about matters of government. They pretended to have book knowledge. They didn't comb their hair. They wore dungarees. Listening to the radio description of a terrorist, I felt shivers running down my spine for I knew a terrorist who lived in our neighbourhood: a man who wore spectacles, didn't comb his hair, wore strange flowing robes and dungarees. He frequently spoke English and cursed a lot. His name was Pascal Gwala,

Another terrorist I recognised was Bob Marley. I had enjoyed dancing to his music at the Mkhwanazi house even though I hadn't known what he was singing about. For some reason I felt an affinity with these terrorists. Gwala in his colourful clothes and carefree lifestyle would saunter down the street hurling insults at Buthelezi and at something he called "the system". This appealed to me. Perhaps I would be a terrorist when I grew up.

My only reservation was that terrorists, according to the radio, killed people, ate their hearts and livers, and drank their blood. While I enjoyed boiled goat or ox blood, and had a taste for different kinds of meat, human flesh did not appeal to me.

Inkatha, however, gained support at the expense of the terrorists. Although the organisation had launched as a cultural organisation intent on reviving Zulu customs, traditions and pride, it had gradually become political. People had to join or risk expulsion from their township. When I joined the Boy Scouts, we marched to songs in praise of Buthelezi and Inkatha.

*"Singamasosha eNkatha; singamasosha eNkatha . . ."*

(We are the soldiers of Inkatha; we are the soldiers of Inkatha . . .)

Inkatha had such support and popularity and was so cut off from the rest of the country that when the Soweto uprising took place in June 1976, we hardly noticed.

Those who listened to the radio learned that black children were being killed by the police in a place called Soweto. They heard that these

73

children did not want to be taught in Afrikaans. Even then, the Soweto
story was talked about in whispers because the subject was taboo, an
act of disseminating communist and terrorist propaganda. But then,
Soweto was remote and we had other matters on our minds.

Among these were the kidnapping and killing of young children. It
was said that the kidnappers drove about in a black hearse with darkened windows. They lured children into the car before driving away
at high speed. Their victims either disappeared or ended up dead in a
gutter. The kidnappers' campaign was called Phungukani MaZulu –
we are reducing the number of Zulus.

To many people this campaign tied in with Buthelezi's theory of a
conspiracy to undermine and decimate the Zulu people.

It was said that Phungukani MaZulu not only had bad medicine, but
also had magic. The Phungukani MaZulu car could change itself into
a frog. It could become a vegetable or an insect. Wherever they went,
children had to be vigilant. And one Saturday morning while I walked
home from the nearby shop Phungukani MaZulu came for me.

I heard a sound in the road behind me and turned to see an onion
rolling in my direction. No matter what I did it followed me. My mind
screamed: Phungukani MaZulu. I ran, and for a moment thought I heard
running feet behind me. Phungukani MaZulu was gaining. I screamed.
The Hadebes shouted why was I screaming and running, I should be
careful of cars.

"Phungukani MaZulu is chasing after me! Help! Help!"

Sweating and breathing heavily, I rushed into our home, locking the
door behind me.

Even though my mother tried to reassure me that Phungukani Ma-
Zulu didn't exist, that it was a scare story to keep children indoors, she
didn't sound convinced. For a start, she couldn't explain the disappear-
ance of some children from their homes.

Decades later I realised the disappearances were linked to the wave
of radicalism that followed the Soweto uprising when scores of children fled into exile to join the guerrilla fighters.

# Soccer wars

EARLY IN 1977 one of the biggest soccer clubs in the township, Three Active United (TAU), was embroiled in internal strife. Some players felt that they were being discriminated against and left to form their own team, Eastern Pirates. The prime movers behind the split were the Dlamini brothers, egged on by their father, once a senior official with TAU. But before Eastern Pirates played their first match, one of the brothers was attacked and brutally beaten. The attackers were supporters of TAU unhappy with the breakaway. Instead of "persuading" the players and supporters of the newly-formed outfit to come back to the TAU fold, the attack led to hostilities when the eldest Dlamini boy declared war on TAU leaders and supporters. He attacked a senior TAU manager one Saturday afternoon, precipitating a bloody war between the two teams. Almost every weekend there would be skirmishes in the streets. Knives and pangas would be pulled, blood would flow.

And the flow lapped against my home. The TAU official who had been attacked by Eastern Pirates lived in our section of the township and was friends with my father. He turned to him for support, suggesting they join forces to attack the leaders and supporters of Eastern Pirates. My father, and his friend and co-manager, Dubazane, refused.

Then the manager of Eastern Pirates visited my father to find out whose side he was on.

"Dlamini," my father said as the two men sat on the lawn outside our house, "I have no fight with anyone. You know as I know that I have never been part of TAU before. Besides, my team is experiencing major financial problems as it is. My own money is running out. I am even considering quitting."

The two men spoke at length in sonorous, sombre tones. By the end of the meeting they had been joined by Dubazane. The upshot was that the two teams – Eastern Pirates and Silver Stars – decided to send a joint delegation to the township's biggest tycoon, Mr Mcoyi, appealing for financial aid. Mcoyi flaunted his wealth by buying expensive cars: a Mustang convertible, a Cadillac, a Ford Barracuda. He built the township's first shopping centre that boasted a huge supermarket, a greengrocer, a restaurant and a liquor outlet. Mcoyi was a big, round man with an ego to match who referred to himself as *uJesu waseMpumalanga*, the Jesus of Mpumalanga.

Because he was rich, people wanted him to stand for mayor, but he scoffed at the idea: "Politics is for poor fools who want to rob ordinary people. If you are rich like me, you don't need to go around begging people for votes. When I want to do something, I just dig into my pocket, and *voila*, all problems are solved."

Besides, Mcoyi was politically astute, wary of becoming a mayor reporting to the racist National Party and its surrogate Inkatha. (Many years later Mcoyi's children would become outspoken critics of apartheid and prominent activists of the ANC. His daughter would die at the hands of Inkatha supporters.)

Figures like Mcoyi inspire as much fear as respect and become the stuff of urban legends. One story had it that he would pace the courtyard in front of his business, occasionally spitting in the face of some poor passer-by then pompously pull out a stash of banknotes and say, "Take this money and wipe your monkey face with it! Maybe some day your children will be as rich as me."

Much to Mcoyi's annoyance, a Mr Langa built the township's first double-storey building. This was a shopping centre with a general dealers downstairs and a restaurant above. Food at the posh restaurant was expensive: a plate of rice and beef stew set you back the equivalent of a loaf of brown bread, a small packet of sugar, a pint of milk and a packet of ten cigarettes.

Mcoyi fumed at this businessman's insolence. *"Ngihleli emzini wami ngiyadla, inja ingibuka ukhakhayi"* – I'm sitting at my posh house, eating my good food, and there's this dog looking down upon me.

But what disturbed Mcoyi the most was the name of Langa's business, *"Qedukwazi"* – I'll teach you a lesson.

Mcoyi fired back by changing the name of his business from the eponymous Mcoyi's Shopping Centre to *"Bakhaliphicebo"* – what are they planning now? To further spite his business adversary, he bought a few more expensive cars, upgraded the restaurant at his shopping centre, and invited well-heeled people from around the province to dine there.

Langa was a quiet, church-going man with a great respect for money. He had made his stash playing the horses, and prior to getting rich had been a close friend of my father's. In fact he had benefited from my father's racing tips, although my father never used his insider knowledge to the same effect. Shortly after Langa opened for business, my father approached him about a sponsorship for the soccer team. Tight-fisted Langa scratched his head and told my father to come back the following week. Inevitably, the following week became the following week. But my tenacious father never gave up until, in exasperation, Langa financed new kit for the Silver Stars. But that was all.

Which was why approaching Mcoyi for a sponsorship appealed to my father. He wanted to spite Langa who was spitting in the faces of his former friends.

My father, his co-manager and Dlamini duly arrived at Mcoyi's house and were shown into the lounge by a servant. There they waited until Mcoyi whirled in, swigging from a beer jug and belching. He shook hands with his guests.

"So, my people, what can Mcoyi do for you?"

Dlamini explained the proposal in detail. Mcoyi nodded, shifting luxuriously in his huge sofa, enjoying his beer. Once Dlamini had finished, Mcoyi called for food and refreshments. Mounds of meat and rice and salads were served. Beer flowed. The men conversed excitedly about the sponsorship, and it indeed looked like Mcoyi, the big fish, was biting.

The merrymaking was at its zenith when Mcoyi, beer in hand, his face beaming with joy, got up and said, *"Ah, ngiyajabula uma ngibona izinja zami zidla. Busani zinja, uMcoyi usaphila."* Ah, it gives me great pleasure to see my dogs eating. You must celebrate, my dogs, while Mcoyi is still alive.

Commotion suddenly exploded with Dlamini rising from the sofa, a knife in his hand.

"*Ah, mfana, nc nc nc,*" Mcoyi clucked. "*Ufuna ukubulala uJesu wase-Mpumalanga?*" Ah, boy, you want to kill Jesus of Mpumalanga?

My father's delegation left in a huff, despite Mcoyi's attempts to pacify them. "Come back, you men," he called out. "I'll give you all the money you need. Don't go to that fool Langa! Come back!"

The next tycoon that my father's delegation visited was a quiet man called Rodger Dinga Sishi, who had recently opened a petrol station. Sishi was not a newcomer to Mpumalanga. He had grown up in the area long before the township was built. As a young man he'd been a teacher, before moving to Johannesburg to help manage Orlando Pirates. But once the soccer wars started in Johannesburg, he returned to his roots.

Sishi was a portly, ever-smiling man with a surprisingly tiny squeaky voice that belied his size. He listened to my father's delegation, nodded sagely and said he would consider their request. A few weeks later, he formed his own soccer team – Isikhalo se-Afrika – with a consortium of other business people. Because Isikhalo had money, it managed to steal many players from my father's Silver Stars.

My father had to act or the team would collapse. He merged his club with another up-and-coming side called Crocodiles but, unfortunately, the name my father had cherished for many years disappeared, the Silver Stars became the Crocodiles. This loss drove him to serious drunken binges.

But there was an upside. The new outfit attracted a number of sponsorships from businessmen outside the township. As a result, Crocodiles could buy some of the best players and because of that it performed well. However, my father had lost control of the team and that caused him great pain. His co-manager and co-owner was a lanky affable man called Cox Mngoma, a former player of legendary brilliance, now equally famous for his false eye. Often when Mngoma got excited during a soccer game, his false eye fell out of its socket.

"Hey," he would shout, "where's my eye? Boys, come help me find my eye." When the wayward eye was found, he would wipe it on the seat of his pants or lick it clean before putting it back into the empty socket. On his drunken binges my father loved telling stories about his friend's errant eye.

Sometimes, after a night's drinking, he would come home late singing songs from his rural past. The bedroom door would be kicked open and he would wake us, insisting that we swear undying loyalty to the Crocodiles.

"Come on my crocodiles," he would slur, using his hands to imitate the movement of a crocodile's jaws. "You are the crocodiles of the future, you're going to crush the enemy with your strong jaws, gulp the enemy, and spit him out. Bloody Mngoma wants to run the club by himself, yet he cannot even see properly! One of these days I am going to kick him in his seeing eye, I promise you. My boys, you promise you will help your father fight the battle for the control of the Crocodiles alone?"

"Yes, we promise," we would chorus, although I had lost all interest in soccer.

# Two donkeys and an ass

APART FROM SOCCER and the cultural traditions which my father drummed into my head, he also instilled in me a love of fishing.

"Fishing is not only fun, but it also provides you with food," he would say. "Clever people believe that the beginning of wisdom is not to give a person a piece of fish but to teach him how to fish."

Buoyed by this belief, he took me to Umncadodo Dam, on the outskirts of the Hammarsdale industrial area. It wasn't big but it teemed with barbel, bass, eel and minnows. It was also a recreational spot for whites. I hadn't seen white people in a long time, not since the days of the Jockeys' Academy.

Although there were no policemen or notices enforcing racial segregation, we kept to our side of the dam and they kept to theirs.

But children being children we crossed the borders and hovered around the white side, hoping to grab sandwiches and morsels of food which the crazy overfed white people habitually threw into the rubbish bins. The white boys, on the other hand, ventured to our side of the dam because they were curious about our home-made fishing rods fashioned from bamboo sticks, fishing line and hooks made from pieces of wire. The white boys carried genuine over-the-counter fishing rods. But we caught as many fish as they did. These cross-border explorations sometimes ended in fist fights and stone throwing, but only when the fighting became too dangerous did the adults intervene.

When my fishing skills improved my father gave me his fishing rod, a real one like those owned by the white boys. My chest swelled with pride. I was a proper fisherman, except I didn't have sandwiches to throw into the rubbish bin.

One summer holiday we were fishing as usual when some of the boys decided to swim, and stripped and plunged naked into the water. The whites, on their side of the dam, threw stones, angry that our splashing about was scaring the fish away. Eventually my friends relented and got out of water. The slanging match and the stone throwing stopped, but now the white boys threatened us with three big dogs.

We, too, had dogs, those thin mongrels that survive by scavenging at dump yards and sewage dams. Suddenly the white boys' terrier pounced on one of the mongrels, sunk his teeth in and dragged the undernourished bag of bones towards the water's edge. The white boys cheered. "Go for him, Rex! Kill him! Eat him! Kill."

We were silent, watching the dog mauling the poor little creature. Then a mongrel jumped on the back of the terrier and we cried out enthusiastically, "Go for him, John Tate." (A few weeks previously we'd seen a boxing match between a black American called Big John Tate and South Africa's heavyweight champion, Gerrie "Boksburg Bomber" Coetzee. To see a black man whipping a white man had warmed our hearts.) So did the performance of the poor undernourished mongrel which was hanging onto the throat of the terrier, as it staggered about bleeding and foaming at the mouth.

One of the white boys took his sjambok and whipped the small dog. But the dog wouldn't budge. The white boy started crying, and eventually the mongrel let go. The terrier collapsed, panting.

We were in trouble. The police station wasn't far from the dam. The police would be here in a minute. They would surely take us in for pitting the dogs against each other. We had killed a white man's dog. Fortunately nothing came of the event. Except John Tate notched up another victory.

# Mashicila

GANGS HAVE LONG BEEN A FEATURE of township life. Our township was dominated by the Amakwaitos and the uMsingizane gangs, although there were many others. The threat of the gangs loomed largest on Fridays, payday. People were mugged and stabbed and killed. Cries for help mingled with the merrymaking in the shebeens. Soon the gangs were a law unto themselves, terrorising the community. They demanded "protection fees" from businessmen, and those who refused were burgled repeatedly. They even charged a toll at night at a bridge that linked two sections of the township. To this day, the bridge is called kwa-Five Rand. On Monday mornings bodies floating in the stream underneath the bridge were a common sight for children crossing to school. Nor were the police, stationed in white Hammarsdale, interested in the gang violence. They only came into the township to collect corpses.

Something had to be done to stop this scourge of violence. Councillors affiliated to Inkatha took the law into their hands. They formed a vigilante group called Oqonda ("straighten up"), and patrolled the streets at night, armed with knobkerries, sjamboks and, sometimes, spears. They declared a curfew. Anyone on the streets after eight-thirty would be beaten up unless he had good reason for being out. Oqonda's activities then spread into the domestic arena. Men who assaulted their wives were handed over to the caring hands of Oqonda and their kangaroo courts. Or, if your neighbour caused trouble like playing his music too loudly, you dangled the threat of Oqonda and he would, invariably, "straighten up".

Oqonda soon saw to it that the gangsters' reign of terror ended. The community sighed in relief. But now Oqonda exhibited their face of menace, flogging people in public, especially youths who had bad things to say about Inkatha. But these incidents aside, peace and order had returned to our streets and with it came a spiritual awakening.

This religious bonhomie dawned when a new preacher, a self-styled "messiah" intent on saving man from himself, arrived with considerable fanfare. His name was Reverend Mashicila. He was portly, wore large spectacles and had a ready smile for everyone. With him was an entourage of workers who pitched his tent in a vacant lot in our section of the township. Officially his church was called Assemblies of God, but we called the place where the congregation gathered to worship eTendeni, the place of the big tent.

Reverend Mashicila's entourage was a mixture of interesting characters. Some were preachers, others sang in the choir. They spoke a number of languages, a clear indication that the Mashicila entourage had been on the road for some time.

For a while the charismatic Reverend Mashicila received the same adulation that had been reserved for Chief Mangosuthu Buthelezi. The man could preach. He could make you feel that you were already in heaven, lounging at the feet of God, sipping milk and honey from the Holy Chalice.

His sermons began in a low-key, conversational, anecdotal way about how as a young man he had robbed and stabbed people. Gradually, the sermon would move into top gear, the congregation right up there with him.

"AND THEN THE LORD SPOKE TO ME, HE SAID, SON, THE LORD SPOOOOKE TO ME, HE SAID, SON, FOR HOW LONG ARE YOU GOING TO KILL YOUR OWN PEOPLE? DON'T YOU KNOW THAT THE FURNACES OF HELL ARE WAITING FOR THE LIKES OF YOU? CAN I GET AN AMEN?"

"AMEN! AAAMEEEEN! HALLELUJAH PRAAAISE THE LORD!"

Then the spirit would possess the people. They pulled at their hair, rolled in the aisles, fainted, soiled their clothes, foamed at the mouth, spoke in tongues. Under Reverend Mashicila's piercing eyes, the lame walked again, the blind could see and the deaf and the mute regained their senses.

Or so it was said.

Well known thugs, their faces marred by scars, came to the tent to "receive Jesus". They climbed the pulpit and told all and sundry how bad they were until Jesus spoke to them. They came with their knives and pangas which they dumped into a huge basket. Ill-begotten goods were brought to the tent. And then over the weekend these wheelbarrows, spades, pick-axes, packets of cement stolen from the construction company that was busy building the township would be jettisoned into the Umlazi river which uncomplainingly swallowed the rewards of sin. Afterwards, the good Reverend would plunge his new recruits into the water and baptise them.

Reverend Mashicila had another message too, a message told in movies. Watching a movie was a novel experience for many of us and we didn't understand much of what we saw as the movies were in English. Mostly the movies showed people from countries such as Mozambique, Rhodesia, Ethiopia. Black people killing one other. Black people starving, children with distended bellies and rickety legs. People were suffering in those countries. And then the movies would show black South Africans smiling, happy as they moved into their new houses in the townships that were springing up everywhere. How lucky the black South African people were to have a government that cared for them, a government that provided them with security and shelter.

But it wasn't the movies so much as the music that drew us to The Tent. Mashicila had a band that belted out hot American spirituals as if the musicians were from the Deep South. On Wednesday and Friday nights we rollicked to the music.

*Rrrride on Moses, riiide on King Emmanuel, I want to see my Jesus in the morning . . .*

Or it would be the riveting:

*He calmed the ocean, my Lord, yes he did, yes he did.*
*He calmed the raging sea, yes he did, yes he did.*
*Jesus says Peter do you love me?*
*Yes, he did, yes he did . . .*

Or:

*Yes, Jesus loves me, yes, Jesus loves me*
*for the Bible says it's so . . .*

We were in heaven. We were with Shadrack, Meshack and Abednego. Abraham, Isaac, Jacob, Mark, Luke, Timothy. All the holy saints and angels flapped about us in the joy and celebration of the Lord. If heaven was like this, I wanted to stay with Reverend Mashicila forever. And some people did. They quit their jobs and offered themselves to the church. My aunt Zodwa was one. She stopped the odd jobs she did for various people, and gave herself body and soul to the Lord, to the service of Reverend Mashicila.

The immense power of Reverend Mashicila's holy words even pierced the stone-hearted Baba Mndaweni, one of our neighbours. He was a senior bricklayer with the construction company LTA. Since I'd known him, Baba Mndaweni had been a hard-drinking gambler who harassed his family relentlessly. He was also a kleptomaniac. He stole wheelbarrows, spades and other tools from his employers to sell them in the township. Almost every household in our section owned a wheelbarrow or some other tool, thanks to Baba Mndaweni's talents. But after just one visit to The Tent, not only did Baba Mndaweni supplicate himself before the mighty frame of Reverend Mashicila, but the next time he went there he brought his whole family: wife, eight children and ageing mother. Baba Mndaweni became a born-again Christian.

He stopped drinking and became a regular at The Tent. One night, with the aid of his sons, he brought four wheelbarrows to the Reverend. Some months before he'd stolen these wheelbarrows from his employers and sold them to neighbours. But when he saw the light, he reclaimed the wheelbarrows and returned the money he'd received for them. It was only right, he told those who had bought the stolen goods. A few days later, on a festive Saturday morning, Reverend Mashicila's flock trekked to the banks of the Umlazi River. Singing "*Akanamandla uSathane*" – Satan is powerless – the jovial congregants helped Baba Mndaweni jettison the wheelbarrows, spades and other implements he'd stolen. The lore of Reverend Mashicila's church dictated that to be cleansed, you literally had to throw away your sins. People whispered that definitely Baba Mndaweni had changed his ways. This was a miracle.

About this time my aunt became a good family friend of the Mnda-wenis, drinking tea and eating bread with them, singing praises to her newly-found Lord.

My father, not a deeply religious man, was disturbed by my aunt's conversion to the born-again church. One night he took one of the great sticks that he armed himself with whenever he ventured out after dark, and rained blows on Aunt Zodwa. "You are making the Khumalo family a laughing stock!" he shouted as he systematically, rhythmically beat the poor woman. "You are poking fun at our religious convictions, con-sorting with shady gods!"

We, the children, cowered in a corner with my mother, watching tear-fully. Like those Biblical figures Shadrack, Meshack and Abednego, Aunt Zodwa didn't wilt under the force of blows but kept repeating that she had found the True and Living God unlike the idols of the Catho-lics which decorated Catholic churches.

In the end she was the victor, and my father did not even carry out his threat to evict her from our house. However, the neighbours heard about the incident and once again the Khumalo household was said to be bewitched.

# Bewitched Again

IT WAS A BEAUTIFUL SUMMER AFTERNOON in 1978. A group of us were swimming in one of the small ponds on the outskirts of the township when I had a tiff with one of the Radebe girls, Maliwase. She was a gangly big-boned girl of about seventeen, a good three and a half years older than me. But I wasn't scared of her. She was a girl.

No doubt in response to an insult she hit me hard in the face. Now a girl can't klap you hard in the middle of the street and get away with it. I hit back with a good punch to the stomach. She doubled over in pain, then came at me with a volley of punches and slaps to my face that made me see stars.

The problem with boys was that we wanted a "fia fayt" – a fair fist fight, clean, organised jabs, well-aimed left and right hooks, round-house kicks – the way they fought in the Bruce Lee and Jackie Chan movies we watched in the school hall on weekends. Girls came at you like enraged beasts, screaming and clawing, pushing and biting.

Under Maliwase's attack I got panicky, giving my punches more bite, more speed. But I was too late. She rammed me with her forehead in the pit of my stomach and I went sprawling. When a boy floors you, he immediately declares his victory, or waits for you to get up. Not so with girls. Maliwase pounced on me, pinned me to the ground with her knees and panel-beat my face. By the time she was through, my nose was bleeding. I got up shamefacedly to loud cheers from the girls. Some of the boys said derisive things about me. Others shook their heads sadly. I had let the side down. By the time I got home, I was crying angrily.

Somewhat later in the day I came across Maliwase in the street. Now, I had a reputation for never giving up and Maliwase knew that. On the occasions I lost fist fights I would challenge the bully to a stick fight. I never lost any of these. Maliwase saw me and ran. I wasn't carrying sticks but I was carrying a knife. I caught up with her and started whacking her back, her buttocks, her arms. An older neighbour came to her rescue and pulled us apart, depriving me of my knife. The matter was amicably settled but word was soon out that the Khumalo boy had not behaved like his usual quiet self. He had almost killed a girl. He was possessed. He had been bewitched.

A few months later something horrible happened to me. I woke with my body itching painfully, especially around my crotch and in my armpits. Hundreds of tiny bugs stubbornly stuck to my pubic area. I wanted to scream. I had heard about pubic lice from older boys. It was something you contracted after sleeping with "a bad girl". Yet I had not slept with a girl in my life.

When my father came home I told him everything. Had I slept with a girl? I replied, no. At first he didn't believe me, but eventually he was convinced and gave me an interesting theory which held that a witch could place a line of lice in your path and once you stepped over this invisible line, the lice jumped for your pubic area. My lice, however, were also in my eyelashes and on my head. My father visited a herbalist and returned with herbs and powders that I had to drink, bath in, and use as an enema. The itching soon went away.

My mother had watched these proceedings with fascination. Once the herbs were finished she took me to a doctor who prescribed some ointments and tablets. Enough of this pagan mumbo jumbo, she muttered to herself.

# Piwe's cultural weapon

PENIS SIZE IS AN ISSUE FOR MANY MEN. Those which look like knobkerries are associated with power and patriarchy in Zulu culture. At school, a boy with a big dick twisted like a wild banana was revered and envied by both sexes.

In our neighbourhood the luckiest guy was Piwe Masinga. We started school together, played soccer together, shot birds together in the bushes beyond the township. Piwe was a Shangaan. His father had come from Mozambique and was one of the first citizens of the township. However, Shangaans were few and far between and there were many myths about their culture. That they were a close-knit community did not help dispel these myths. Besides, Zulus looked down on them. A joke went: "Eyi, I saw a horrific car accident yesterday. Three people and one Shangaan were killed." But although Shangaans were mocked in most things, the men were respected when it came to discussions of penis sizes.

I have never seen a Shangaan man with a small or average penis. They have large cultural weapons. By the time Piwe was twelve years old, he had a member that many men would have envied.

One explanation for the endowment of Shangaan men has it that when a Shangaan boy is born, the father plants a tree at a secret place, and, as the sacred tree grows, so will the boy's penis. When the father is satisfied that his boy's penis is an acceptable size, he chops down the tree.

"You see how big I am," Piwe would brag when we admired the few centimetres he had gained since the last measuring. "And this is only the beginning. My father still hasn't chopped off my tree. I still have a few centimetres to gain. Just watch me, you Zulu boys."

What would happen, I wondered, if Piwe's tree was washed away in a flood. Surely this would spell disaster for our friend Piwe, I would say, to uproarious laughter. Imagine him running around with a member that refused to stop growing, crying out, "Where's my tree? Has anyone seen my pipi tree!"

But while I made fun of Piwe, I had problems of my own: acne. My face was suffused with pimples, and girls wouldn't speak to me. My mother said not to worry, it was a passing phase, and gave me soaps and other ointments, but they didn't help.

"The reason he is having so many pimples is because he has never had a woman," it was whispered about me.

"Yah, I hear that large deposits of sperm in a person's body don't only cause pimples, but they can also interfere with your brain cells. Your mind becomes slower. Sometimes you can even go blind. Vusi must stop being an Arab." (An Arab was a boy who was stingy with his sperm. At the time Arabs were regarded as being stingy with their oil.)

Enter now my Aunt Theresa who worked as a domestic servant for a white family in Umhlanga Rocks. Her daughter had recently moved in with us so Aunt Theresa visited at least once a month. She was a charming woman with a ready smile and her visits caused a stir. Resplendent in a tight-fitting white skirt which rode just above her knees and a sleeveless orange top, she walked tall on thin stiletto heels, leaving young men gaping in her wake. Her complexion was a high yellow, her lips painted red in a perpetual pout. When she laughed – which she did a lot – her breasts danced, threatening to break free from her bra.

My aunt brought me second-hand clothes from her white employers and would often find time to talk to me. She liked the fact that I was usually to be found sitting quietly with my nose buried in a book.

On this occasion she said, "*Mntakabhuti* [my brother's son], you are becoming a man now. I can see from the pimples on your face and the subtle change to your voice that you are entering another stage in your life. There are things that you now need to learn."

She paused. "You must now take care of yourself, be careful what you wear, watch the way you walk, take heed of the things you say with your mouth. Carry yourself with pride and confidence in public. A man must walk and talk with pride."

Probably my father should have told me these things, but whenever my mother whispered to him that he should talk to me about entering a new stage of life, he would say, "Eish! Dubazane is waiting for me. We have to go fishing." Or: "Eish! The boys are waiting for me. We have to go for soccer training."

Now my aunt patiently explained that I had to change my wardrobe, my manner of speech, and stop playing marbles and other childish games for I was being watched by potential *makotis*.

"But how do I change my wardrobe when my parents can't even afford to buy me the compulsory set of schoolbooks?" I asked.

"Use your head," she replied. "You don't have to be from a family where they drink their tea from china cups to dress in a manner that's acceptable to the ladies. And, by the way, this is no licence for you to give people's daughters unwanted babies, you hear?" And she laughed loud and long.

If only she knew that I was a harmless Arab.

She then said that many white families in Umhlanga Rocks were in need of reliable "garden boys". But that was a distance away so instead I found a job with an Afrikaans family, the Van Rensburgs, in a white suburb that was easier to reach. At the end of my first day they fired me for working like a sissy.

"I want strong boys," said Van Rensburg, touching his biceps.

"Yes, sir," I said meekly.

"And don't you bloody sir me! I am baas to you, you hear?"

"Yes . . ."

"Yes what?"

"Yes baas, yes baas," I said hurriedly, scared of the violence in the man's voice.

"I want strong boys who can work fast. And you can't work fast. I want boys who can push the blerry grass machine like real men, not sissies. Go home and sit in your mother's lap!" He gave me R3 for my efforts.

In the train home I asked the other boys what was wrong with calling a white man sir.

"A white man you work for is not sir, he is baas."

"But that's not the English they teach us at school."

"Your teacher is sir, but a white man is baas."

"In fact the auntie who works in the kitchen of my white people calls the white man master."

"Other people call their bosses my lord."

"Call them anything but sir . . ."

I was not impressed.

The following Saturday I was on the streets again, energetically looking for a white family in need of a boy. I needed the money. I could imagine myself sauntering down my street resplendent in the fashionable garb of the day: shiny Dobbshire slacks and thick-soled Florsheim shoes, Pringle cardigans, elegant Viyella shirts.

I landed a job with a kind couple who had two teenage sons and a daughter. They were soft-spoken people who didn't mind being called sir and madam. Their surname was Fox. Unlike my first employer, they even asked me my full name.

"Frederick Khumalo, sir," I said proudly.

"Are you Moselekatse then?" the man said.

Initially, I couldn't figure out what he was talking about, then realised that he was referring to my heroic ancestor, Mzilikazi.

The man explained in detail what was expected of me, told me my salary would be R8 a day – a princely sum. After three Saturdays I would have saved enough to buy my first outfit: a pair of Triple Seven pants at R21, and a Blue Diamond T-shirt at R5. Some months later my wardrobe had changed but the girls still weren't biting. My pimpled face remained a turnoff and my self-esteem suffered.

After school, I began frequenting the Mkhwanazi house. The eldest boy was a dagga merchant with an assortment of friends and hangers-on, some of whom were known criminals. Having been rejected by my peers of both sexes, I began to ingratiate myself with this crowd. The lovely thing about dagga smokers is that they don't care about your looks. Apart from the criminals, there were a host of teachers, gamblers, soccer players and plain ordinary people who sought out the

Mkhwanazi house. This egalitarian community of smokers loved jazz and reggae music, and it was here that I first heard the likes of organist Jimmy Smith, saxophonists Big John Patton and Stanley Turrentine, and of course, Bob Marley.

But while the smokers' club liked music, they had an aversion to the female sex.

The guys would be sitting on the lawn, a burning chalice of the holy herb passing among them, when a girl in all her finery would come sashaying up the street.

"Ag, look at that bitch," somebody would say, "look at how she's swaying her hips. She thinks we are interested in her."

"All a bitch like this wants from you is your money. If you don't have money, she wrinkles her uppity nose at you. Bloody creatures from hell, am I wrong, gents?"

"The bloody things will give you diseases as well."

"Hey, wena," somebody would suddenly shout at the hapless woman, "don't ever walk in this street again, you hear? We don't want temptresses and bitches like you in this neighbourhood."

Initially I was shocked by these utterances, but soon got used to this manner of talking. After all I was a victim of rejection and I felt an affinity with these brothers.

Babo Mkhwanazi brought his supplies from a nearby farm in a number of huge sacks. In turn, he would supply small-time dealers, and used runners to ensure that his contacts were well supplied. I started working for him as a runner, delivering parcels of dagga. It was also the runner's job at the end of the month to "remind" tardy customers to settle their bills. Reminding meant slapping the customer around.

One of the guys who frequented Babo's place was Step-by-Step, a Shangaan with a penchant for quoting Bob Marley's songs. He also reminded us that although it was good to consume dagga and get high, we shouldn't forget our responsibility to the nation and generations to come.

"One day when you die, Steve Biko who died for you will want to know what you did for the black nation."

"Talk, Step-by-Step, talk!" he would be urged.

"Dagga is not the answer to our problems. We should read, gentlemen, read and preach the word of liberation."

"*Ah, usuyanya-ke manje* – you are talking shit now. You can't insult the holy herb. This talk of politics is driving you insane. Don't mix politics with insults about our holy herb. If you know what's good for you, just stop talking your politics now and show us your big Shangaan dick!"

Guffaws of laughter.

Apart from books and magazines which he always carried around, Step-by-Step was a great lover of radio and a prolific contributor to Radio SR's special request programme. Almost every night an announcer would read a postcard greeting from our own Step-by-Step. It made us feel good that we knew a guy whose name was regularly mentioned on an English-language radio station broadcasting all the way from Johannesburg. Step-by-Step was also the first to introduce us to Radio Freedom. This short-wave station was the mouthpiece of the banned ANC. Its broadcast opened with the blood-curdling bark of automatic gunfire, and the angry words "war against the apartheid regime". The station, Step-by-Step would explain, was broadcasting from somewhere in the bush, run by people he called Freedom Fighters.

"The system calls them *amaphekulazikhuni* – terrorists – but we should call them freedom fighters because they have fled into exile in order to bring us freedom from the white man."

"You educated people," someone interjected derisively, "you will get us into trouble with the white man. The white man will one day just kill us all because you are irritating him with your political talk. I am telling you now that we will never win this war against the white man. He's too . . ."

"Oh, there goes another Shangaan!" somebody interrupted. "If you Shangaans want to fight among yourselves, go back to Mozambique and finish your war over whose penis is bigger."

Ethnic jokes were commonplace. But beneath the humour lurked the venom of tribalism and chauvinism. Apartheid had indoctrinated us into looking down upon each other: we were tribes of varying degrees of intelligence and civilisation, the system said. The Shangaans were stupid and uncivilised, the Zulus bloodthirsty, and the Xhosas sly jackals ready to strip you of your clothes. We believed that the Xhosa regarded everyone's property as their own.

At some point, Step-by-Step loaned me a magazine called *Frank Talk*. The writers used words such as "scientific socialism", "black consciousness", "vanguard of the struggle". These were new concepts and I needed a dictionary to make sense of them. One article, however, told the life story of Stephen Bantu Biko, who had died after torture by white security policemen not many months before, and I was captivated.

Another of the magazines was *Pace*, a colourful magazine with pictures of beautiful semi-nude girls on the cover. Inside were fascinating stories of gangsters and the who's who of black high society. The magazine ran profiles on doctors, lawyers, writers, and told of how they beat the system and how they negotiated themselves out of poverty. Of course, hard-core political guys such as Step-by-Step complained that *Pace* and its ilk were lulling black people into complacency, suggesting that they could become successful despite the system. But how could the system be so bad if it allowed a Richard Maponya to build a business empire or Tamsanqa Kambule to be a professor of mathematics at the predominantly white University of the Witwatersrand?

I found *Pace* refreshing. Ordinarily, black people did not feature in mainstream magazines and newspapers. The only time you saw a black person in the media was if he was a criminal or a government-appointed councillor. So I found the profiles of Professor Kambule and Bishop Desmond Tutu encouraging. Clearly it was possible to fight my way out of poverty by working hard at school, although an education was no guarantee that you would escape apartheid violence. *Pace* also showed me that in America, despite inherent flaws and racism in the society, some black people were making it. I read about Booker T Washington, Martin Luther King Jr, Marvin Gaye, Curtis Mayfield, Bob Marley, Marcus Garvey, Arthur Ashe, Harry Belafonte, Malcolm X – black people who had spoken out against oppression.

Once my mother found me engrossed in an article about an American group called the O'Jays who were on their way to perform in South Africa. I had heard the group on the radio and longed to see them live. "I see you like the O'Jays?" she said.

I replied enthusiastically, then pointed out that *Pace* said we should boycott the concert. My mother agreed. "You'll get to see better music from your very own country in the near future," she said. "Next month they are having a music festival at Kings Park stadium. I'll take you there."

I was stunned! "But, Ma, we are struggling financially. We are deep in poverty."

"Never tempt God, because he will give you exactly what you're asking for – starvation and poverty."

The next month, my mother kept her promise. We took a train to Durban, walked from Durban central station to the stadium where things were happening. Here I was watching the big names: Philip Tabane and Malombo, Papa and Blondie Makhene, Era, Margaret Singana, Neville Nash, Richard Jon Smith. I couldn't thank my mother enough.

"If you're a hard-working good boy, you'll get rewarded," was her simple response.

I threw myself back into my books. *Pace* profiled Alex Haley, describing his excruciating exercise of finding out who he really was, a journey that took him back to the Gambia where his ancestors had been enslaved. His tale, an excerpt of which was published in the magazine, left an indelible mark on me. I came to respect the power of the written word, the sacredness of heritage, and the importance of knowing one's history. How else are you to face the future if you don't appreciate the past? As Haley wrote in *Roots*:

". . . three groups of people lived in every village. First were those you could see – walking around, eating, sleeping, and working. Second were the ancestors, whom Grandma Yaisa had now joined. And the third people – who are they?" asked Kunta.

'The third people,' said Omoro, 'are those waiting to be born.'"

But my favourite column in *Pace* was High Voltage, written by Vusi Khumalo. His work fascinated me partly because I was his namesake, but more particularly because he was funny, always cheekily poking fun at the white government and the black stooges of apartheid. I remember a piece on Chief Patrick Mphephu, the "prime minister" of the Venda homeland. Mphephu was quoted telling his people that he was ready to take his homeland into "independence" from the white Pretoria government.

"Transkei did it," he said pompously. "Ciskei did it. Bophuthatswana did it. So why can't we did it?"

From the day the column was published, Mphephu came to be known as Prime Minister Did It Mphephu, and Venda became Did It homeland.

In days to come, Step-by-Step was to tell me more about the political struggle and to broaden my education. In days to come, Step-by-Step was to give me more magazines and books to read. I took to listing all the new English words I encountered in a notebook. Next to each new word I wrote the meaning which I then memorised. In days to come, I would use all the new words in my school essays, or English compositions as they were called.

Step-by-Step brought more books, one by James Hadley Chase. Now these books were exciting with sexy titles such as *No Orchids For Miss Blandish*. Reading these books was like watching gangster movies. The action was palpable. When everybody was asleep, I read a James Hadley Chase deep into the night until my mother complained that I was using up her candles with my never-ending reading.

One of the most intriguing books from Step-by-Step's stash was *Animal Farm*. I read it repeatedly although Step-by-Step decided that I was too young or illiterate to understand the deeper meaning of this powerful book. He called it a satire.

I do believe the saying that if you want to hide something from a black person, put it in a book. The more I read, the more I realised that books carried potent secrets. Profiles of Frederick Douglass, Richard Wright, Martin Luther King Jr told me that no oppressor could sit on the lid of a boiling pot forever. Visionary, courageous, dedicated black people such as these became an inspiration to me. Their pronouncements helped me to dream big, to embrace a happy, courageous future. Sometimes these dreams looked like mirages, but they kept the hope alive despite the suffering. Books and magazines were an escape. I enjoyed movies, but books opened worlds. They taught me discipline. They taught me to think and imagine. In my mind I travelled the world. Because of my obsessive book reading, I lived inside my head most of the time. But I knew that many of my peers thought my aloofness and absent-mindedness had to do with dagga.

Step-by-Step was a blessing: a breath of fresh air, an innocent, fun-loving, argumentative young man among smokers that included the downtrodden and the criminals. But as much as I was a reader, I was also a teenager with a need to belong. Before I knew it, I had joined one of the pickpocketing crews. It was difficult not to.

Although I carried a knife, I never used it on a "corpse", as we called a person we intended to rob. There were many ways of doing the job. For example, a number of us would mingle with the crowds at the busy taxi rank in Hammarsdale. One method was to slit open a victim's purse or trouser pocket with a razor blade, take out the money and immediately pass it to an accomplice, who handed it to another gang member, spiriting it away. If we were caught in the act, we fled. I was never caught, but then I was small and droopy-eyed, looking like the squarest of squares.

Another, riskier operation was to lurk in the shadows near a bus stop. Drunks or people too fat to run were our victims. We would follow someone into the darkness, hit him *ijombolo*-style with a short piece of iron on the back of the neck. The victim would collapse unconscious; we would empty his pockets. Alternatively, one of the bigger guys would crook an arm around the victim's neck while the others went through the choking man's pockets.

Daring gangs such as the MaHarangu of Umlazi used to pounce on train passengers. In groups of up to twenty strong they would burst into a carriage, armed with huge knives and pangas. At the next station they were out and onto a train headed in the opposite direction, leaving tears and blood in their wake.

These were also people I looked up to, people I took pride in knowing even at a distance. Because knowing them was cool, something to boast about.

"We are sitting under the peach tree playing cards, when mChina suddenly walks into the yard with his posse . . ."

"Which mChina? Mchina with the funny eyes?"

"Yep! The one and only."

"What knife was he carrying this time?"

"Of course he doesn't go around brandishing a knife."

"But people say he is always carrying a knife?"

"They call him the man with eleven fingers because he is so fast at drawing you would think the knife was part of his hand."

"But now, how do you get to hang around with people like him?"

"It depends on who you are, what you do, understand?"

And there I would leave it. You had to keep them guessing, you had to cultivate respect. Your boys had to know that you were not just a school-going moegoe, you were down with the brothers in the hood. Boys who were serious about the street couldn't be equally serious about school. Even though you were enjoying school, you had to show that school was a place to pass the time while you planned big things for the street.

# A dangerous corpse

WHEN MY WARDROBE CHANGED DRASTICALLY, my mother wanted to know where the money came from. If she couldn't afford to buy my school books and stationery, how could I? I told her I earned the money from gardening. This was partly true, but the bulk came from my nocturnal assignments on Fridays.

I know very few black male South Africans my age who were not, at one stage or another, pickpockets or knife-wielding muggers. Gangsterism and crime are part of township life. Not because black people are inherently criminal but because they are driven to crime out of desperation. Over the years the gangs became sophisticated and more brutal. Because the crime dons had easy access to large amounts of money, they became role models in their communities. Young people growing up without real role models such as lawyers, teachers, doctors looked up to the gangsters.

After all, standing on street corners smoking and talking with the boys gave you a sense of belonging. And petty crime provided the necessary pocket money for entertaining girls. You also needed money for "jewish" – fancy clothes bought from such Jewish stores as Levisons.

At Phezulu High School I shared a desk with a quiet, brooding, well-dressed character called Nhlanhla. He was feared by both students and teachers because he carried a huge knife. A type of knife known as "Seven Years", because being caught with such a big knife could land you a jail sentence of up to seven years. Nhlanhla did not bother to hide his knife. In fact he would walk into the class and plunge the blade violently into the top of the desk.

The first term had already started when I was transferred from A class to C class, "to inspire slow learners" as my teachers explained. Because there was no other free spot, I ended up next to Nhlanhla.

Nhlanhla was perturbed that I was not scared of him. Others had

refused to share his desk. And although he had never threatened anyone, his mere presence was a threat. He would walk into class late, his
eyes bloodshot, squeeze into the desk and turn round to survey the
class. No one met his eye, nor did the teacher expect an apology. "How-
zit," he would say to me.

"*Moja, outie,*" I would respond.

Then he bumped into me one day in the toilets where I was cleaning
my dagga pipe.

"Why didn't you tell me you smoked?"

"You never asked."

"Where are you from?"

We talked, he mentioned a number of hoodlums from my part of the
township. When he was satisfied that I knew them, and that I was connected to a "merchant", we became friends. I soon learned that he was
also a pickpocket with a violent temper and that he had stabbed many
people while robbing them.

That did not faze me. I had shared dagga pipes with hardened criminals. But when he asked me to join his crew because they had moved
into the big time – robbing banks – and needed more members, I realised that I was moving in the wrong circles. I told him I wasn't interested. Nhlanhla was disappointed but shrugged it off and our friend-
ship endured largely because I had opened new political vistas for him.
I lent him books on the political struggle which I had, in turn, acquired
from Step-by-Step. We had deep discussions on political theory – *uku-
rhabulisana*, as we called it – and, more importantly, I helped him
with his homework.

One Monday, Nhlanhla did not turn up for school. I was concerned.
From his younger brother I learned that he had been stabbed badly
during a fight among the crew over some money they had scored. Nhlanhla almost died, but the experience changed his life. He quit smoking,
both cigarettes and dagga, stayed away from the bottle, and devoted
his attention to a girl he would marry.

On the other hand, another schoolfriend in Nhlanhla's old gang was
shot dead during a bank robbery a few months later.

Meanwhile, my pickpocketing activities continued. One Friday night my neighbour Ntinti and his crew were working Esihohobeni bus stop. Three of them followed a "corpse" into a darkened alley. They moved in. Ntinti, a short strong youngster, crooked his arm around the corpse's neck and pressed a blade into the man's side, shouting, "Give it up! Give me your fucking wallet!" The other two soldiers joined in. But the corpse kicked one in the groin, and in the fracas Ntinti pressed the blade home. But the corpse fought back, winding Ntinti who dropped his knife but kept his hold round the man's neck. Despite the wound and the choke-hold, the corpse staggered down the alley, Ntinti dangling in mid-air, crying out, *"Ngilekeleleni ba'fethu! Lesidumbu sizongibulala"* – Help me, brothers! This corpse is going to kill me.

His comrades left him to his fate. The following day Ntinti was the butt of many jokes at the merchant's house.

"How can you allow yourself to be dragged by a corpse, *mfanakithi?*" they wanted to know.

"Eyi, man, we underestimated that corpse. When I tried to stab him, he elbowed me hard in my tummy. And he grabbed my wrist and twisted it. It was like being caught by a vice grip. And he literally carried me home."

Guffaws of laughter.

"And when we finally got to his house, he pinned me to the ground and worked on me with his shoes."

"You know his house? Why don't we go there now and teach him a lesson. He's setting a bad precedent. Other corpses will lose respect for us. Let's pay him a visit . . ."

*"Ek se, bolova,* look here, guys, count me out."

More laughter, amid a cloud of dagga smoke.

The next Monday he wasn't at school because the corpse had given him a black eye.

After Nhlanhla's experience and Ntinti's encounter with the corpse, I gradually extracted myself from the crew and sought refuge in the comforting safety of my mother's kitchen. This also earned my mother's praises for being a well-behaved boy in a depraved neighbourhood.

If I asked for money to go to a music festival, for example, she wouldn't hesitate in giving me her last cent. The kitchen also gave me a place to read and write.

One of my early efforts was a play – a Jim-comes-to-town tale about a God-fearing man corrupted by the city into crime. Of course the moral of the story was that crime doesn't pay. The play might have been a terrible cliché, but it was performed to hundreds of schoolchildren who seemed to enjoy it.

# Stingy Arab no more

I WAS JUST ABOUT TO KNOCK OFF from my gardening job at the Fox's property one Saturday afternoon when their son Percival called out, "Hey, Frederick, come with me?"

I cursed under my breath but went with him nevertheless. His face was flushed and he wouldn't look me in the eye. Percival was almost my age. Though I resented being ordered around by him, I had no choice in the matter. I was a servant of the family. I was paid to cut the grass, prune the flowers and trees, sweep up dogshit, clean the pool – one of my favourite jobs because I could ogle at madam in her skimpy bikini, her smooth white thighs spread out carelessly as she sunbathed next to the pool. I wondered what Percival wanted with me, especially as he was the quiet type, always sitting under a tree, his nose in a book.

He took me to what the Fox family called the maid's quarters even though they didn't have a maid. Here they stored books, tools and all kinds of unused household items. My heart sank. The bloody brat wanted me to clean this untidy room. I looked at my plastic wristwatch. It was 3.30, thirty minutes before my official *shayile*-time. I wouldn't be able to get anywhere near finishing the job in half an hour.

Percival broke into my angry thoughts, "Do you have a girl, Frederick?"

What is this, I wondered? Was he saying this because of the pimples, my badge of sex starvation? "Of course I do!" I said. It was a lie, but a self-respecting dude from the township is supposed to have a collection of babes at his beck and call.

"Look at this," he said, paging through one of the magazines he carried.

I was jolted by the images: pictures of naked white women. It was not just the whiteness of their flesh, but the way they were posing, exposing their femaleness in a manner I had never imagined possible, their bodies contorted like those of acrobats I'd seen once at a circus.

"I bet you've never seen anything like this before," he said in a subdued voice.

"No," I croaked. My throat was suddenly dry, my temples pounding. "No, I've never seen anything like this before."

Percival was easy to talk to. Sometimes I forgot he was white and my employer's son. Sometimes, when his parents were away for the day, he would offer me a cold drink, saying, "Frederick, why are you baking yourself in this hot sun? The parents are away, so who are you trying to impress? Sit in the shade and rest a bit before you collapse on account of the heat."

The parents. That's what he called his own parents. His elder sister was at a boarding school and when she came home for holidays she would refer to me as The Boy. She insisted on calling her father The Master. Frederick, the master says you must wash his car. Frederick, the master says you must go buy him some cigarettes. Frederick, the master says you haven't cleaned his garage properly. Frederick, the master says there's dog moosh-moosh all over his lawn. Frederick, the master says you must clean the pool. Frederick, the master says this, the master says that.

Not so with Percival. He was distant and non-committal about everything. A dreamer. Whenever my parents and sometimes my friends accused me of being absent-minded, I used to think of Percival. But that afternoon, as we stood side by side gasping at the images of naked white women, he was not talking dreamily. He was very much alive. I could hear his hurried breathing. I could even hear the exaggerated sounds in his throat as he repeatedly swallowed his saliva.

Then he unzipped his fly and his swollen penis popped out. "Hold here," he said. I jumped in shock. But he was only asking me to hold the magazine that was open at a picture of a white woman with red hair. Even the bush between her thighs was flaming red. I had never before seen the full nakedness of a woman, black or white.

And here I was staring at the nakedness of a white woman. Or rather she was pink, but I wasn't complaining. Instead, I was sweating, my heart pounding.

Percival played with his thing, now swollen and red. I, too, was swelling. Percival moaned softly, head thrown back, eyes closed. Then something squirted out of his thing. It was not urine. It was thick and white. Deposits of it landed on the floor. He sighed deeply.

He didn't have to tell me what to do. I unzipped my fly. He took the magazine from me and flipped to another page, saying, "The redhead is mine, take this blonde."

The blonde was a white woman with golden hair and huge breasts. The mound between her thighs was clean shaven.

That occasion marked the beginning of the end of my status as a stingy Arab. I also decided to look for a recipient of my oil riches rather than waste them on the floor of a dirty room.

Percival and I never spoke about the oil explosion afterwards, but it improved our "relationship". For instance, we found out that we were in the same standard and compared notes. The history syllabus we were doing in standard seven, he had done in standard five. All Percival's textbooks were supplied free by the government, I had buy my own. His teacher-to-pupil ratio was one to forty, mine was one to more than eighty-five.

In the face of the Fox's evident wealth, Percival told me that his family was average. I didn't know what he was talking about. To me all white people were wealthy and upper class. I'd never seen a white family living in a house without electricity, running water and a swimming pool.

This was, in a small way, the beginning of my political awakening. I questioned these inequalities. Why couldn't the government buy books for black children? Some white schools were almost empty, whereas black schools were bursting at the seams. I was amazed while walking through the white suburbs to the Fox's house, where I gardened during my school holidays (which didn't coincide with white school holidays), how few were the number of white pupils at some of the schools.

White schools were evidently rich, housed in modern, electrified buildings, while ours were overcrowded and housed in the shells of old buildings. Why this naked hatred? Why this deliberate oppression?

"My father's got lots of books that you must read if you are looking for answers to these questions you've been asking me, Frederick," Percival explained patiently.

One of the first books that Percival gave me was Alan Paton's *Cry, The Beloved Country.*

But while these injustices bubbled in me, I was putting the money I earned from gardening towards another urgency: losing my virginity. I had managed to make a huge improvement in my wardrobe, my pimples had given me some respite, and it wasn't long before I scored.

Losing my virginity was not a pleasurable experience. A few days afterwards I developed a terrible infection. My manhood became inflamed, and pus oozed from the tip. I walked with difficulty. At night I would lie awake, groaning in agony, staring into the darkness, praying for some respite, listening to my siblings asleep beside me. Their every move caused me great discomfort, pain stabbing through my groin.

Walking to school was painful, my underpants chafed against my genitals. Whenever I tried to pee, I hurt. Urine came out in drops that were so fiery that I had to grip the top of the urinal and grunt in agony.

"Khumalo has crossed the River Jordan!" one of my classmates shouted triumphantly when he saw me going through the excruciating exercise of urinating. "Khumalo has arrived! They have given him the drop."

The drop was the colloquial word for venereal disease. My classmates laughed and clapped, and advised me to visit the clinic and tell the nurses what was wrong. Their advice was good; my ordeal was soon over. The sores around my cultural weapon disappeared.

During my early days of sexual activity I learned of a game called streamlining.

"Vusi," said my neighbour Peni one afternoon, "my parents are away, and I've got somebody coming over to my place later. Do you want to join the guys in a streamline?"

"Sure thing," I said eagerly, even though I had no idea what a streamline was. A man's man knew everything, or if he didn't, he never admitted it. I was prepared to watch how the other guys played this streamlining game and join in nonchalantly, as if I was an old hand.

At the appointed time I joined three other boys at Peni's house.

"Have you ever streamlined before," one asked me.

"What do you think I am? A *bhari* from the sticks?" I retorted.

"If you've done it before, you'll have to go in before me so I can see how it's done," he said pleadingly.

We joined another three boys clustered at the entrance to a bedroom, broad smiles plastered on their faces. I could hear the moans and screams of a woman. After a few minutes, Peni and another boy came out, smiling and zipping up their pants.

It dawned on me what was happening. The guys were jamming a girl. Suddenly scared, I pulled out of line, making an excuse that I needed to go to the loo. The other innocent followed me. We stood at the gate debating what to do. We knew the streamlining could lead to trouble. The sad thing was that the girl was Peni's girlfriend. It turned out that he was punishing her for talking to a guy he didn't like.

Streamlining was a common practice, a form of "punishment". It wasn't considered rape. Rape was associated with physical violence and force. Streamlining was about control. A man must control his women. Girls could be streamlined for drinking, simply to teach them a lesson. And the girls never reported it. I suspect they felt no one would believe them, because being streamlined stigmatised you. "Why did they do it to you, out of all the girls in the township? What wrong did you do? You must have asked for it!"

Streamlining went against the values that had been instilled in me. My father respected my mother and women in general. Of course there had been incidents where my father had lost his temper and hit my mother, but most of the time he restrained himself. Whenever their opinions clashed, they would retreat to the privacy of their bedroom. If my mother continued to raise her voice, my father would emerge from the bedroom, saying, "Eish! Women! I must go for a walk."

On the many occasions that my grandpa visited us, he used to tell me to respect and protect women – my mother, my sister and every other women I encountered in the street.

"Man would be nothing without a woman," he would say, taking a

108

swig of brandy. "We men think we are clever and strong; we are nothing without women. We work hard, yes, but if we don't have women in our lives we drink the money away and approach the following day confused and desperate: what did I do with my money? Women are like an ant – they have the innate ability to prepare for bad times ahead, like an ant which works hard in summer hoarding the food away for the terrible, lean, winter months ahead. Were it not for women, we men would be having a party every day of our lives. Men are like boesmans. They don't think about the future." (There was a racist myth at the time that coloured people lived to drink, or drank to live. It was said that every payday they would drink all their money. So Friday was called Boesmans' Christmas.) "When I was a young man," my grandfather continued, "I was taught to beg a woman for everything. Beg her for love. Beg her to respect you. Beg her for food. Be always on your knees. This is why I get worried that boys of today are stealing the fruit of a woman."

Yet guys felt their manhood was restored by humiliating girls in this manner. And these guys weren't only thugs or from broken families, most of my friends came from solid families where the parents held jobs and went to church. OK, our parents never spent much time with us. In many cases they worked in distant towns and only came home once a week, if you were lucky, or once a month. Such were the dictates of a migrant labour system that wouldn't let them take their children with them into the white man's towns.

But even those of us who lived with both our parents were touched by street life. In some cases it was because the parents never had time to sit down and advise us; in other instances we lived Jekyll and Hyde existences: at home we were angels, but on the streets we fell under the spell of our peers and tried to out-street the streetwise. Streamlining was a by-product of out-streeting the streetwise. In later years streamlining became jackrolling, where girls were forced at gun- or knifepoint to have sex with a stranger. A footnote: by the time Peni turned sixteen he had three children with three different women. His parents took him out of school and forced him to find work to feed his brood.

# Life with the American Dudes

As a teenager who had seen too much crime too early in his life, I decided to concentrate on my studies in the belief that education would be my passport out of the poverty, ignorance and violence of the ghetto. I studied hard. But I also got involved in a new craze sweeping the black townships of Durban.

To call the American Dudes a gang would be a misnomer. They were a subculture that had sprung from the American hip hop movement. America has had a profound effect on black urban culture since the 1950s. In the early 1980s, thanks to television, American pop culture bombarded us and we became an extension of the United States culturally. American Dudes was an embodiment of the dominant pop culture.

When I joined the movement we distinguished ourselves from other subcultures, such as the Mapantsula who wore trousers with stovepipe legs, by wearing tight-fitting Bang-bang jeans, tight-fitting muscle tops and high-heeled Watson or Barker shoes. Our hair would either be done in long bushy Afros or in gleaming curls. Our clothes were always bright – pink, orange, yellow – as if to announce to all and sundry: look at me, I am a cheerful clean boy who doesn't skulk around street corners with those Mapantsulas and tsotsis. Unlike the Mapantsulas and tsotsis whose mission in life was to steal people's money, the American Dudes were a bunch of shallow peaceful boys whose raison d'être was fun, fun and more fun. Those members of the American Dudes already employed worked mainly at record bars or as deejays at top discos. They knew their music and shared it with those of us still at school.

Weekends were for partying. We would hire a minibus taxi and drive from township to township playing disco music on the music system we had clubbed together to buy. People throwing birthday parties would hire us as deejays. And our happy clean image made us popular with the fairer sex. Old ladies were heard to say, "I'd rather my little Mavis were to go out with one of these colourful boys called *amaDudu* than with those knife-wielding tsotsis."

My friend the ex-thug Nhlanhla was impressed with my transformation. And envious of my popularity with the ladies. He wanted to join us but couldn't muster the courage. You had to be brave to be seen in the outfits that we wore. Green, yellow, maroon, powder blue. Outrageous stuff, garish stuff, bright stuff. Earth, Wind and Fire stuff. Michael Jackson (pre-nose job) stuff.

Tsotsis began to hate us. They said we stole their girls. How do you steal a girl? Dating is a two-way process. But they didn't see it this way.

One day I was visiting my latest girlfriend in another section of the township. There I was resplendent in my pink short-sleeved Pierre Cardin shirt with matching pink Christian Dior slacks and maroon-and-navy loafers. As we walked we were accosted by a group of mean-looking young men in *pantsula*-style attire, their trousers hanging so low they could fall off at any moment. There were five of them. All much older than me, and some of them troublesome Mapantsulas.

"Which of the two girls do you choose, Roy?" one of the boys said.

"I think I like the dark-complexioned one in the pink outfit."

I recognised one of the guys as Nyoni Hlongwane, my girlfriend's neighbour. He was my age and we had seen each other in the street and exchanged greetings.

"Guys," he said, "just leave him alone. He hasn't done anything to us. Let him be. If he wants to be a sissy, it's his choice."

Roy glared at Nyoni. "Shut up, you! Or do you also want to be a sissy now?" He turned to me and said, "What colour panty are you wearing, sweetie?"

"Can't you hear he's talking to you?" another one said, and punched me in the mouth. I tasted blood. Although I had chosen the soft American Dudes way, I knew how to protect myself in the street. I reached for my knife and charged forward. They pulled back.

Roy said, "Ah, so Sis Pinky is not a sissy after all. Let's see what he's got."

They all reached for their knives.

Decency and caring for my beloved girlfriend flew out the window as I fled. I might have looked like a sissy, but I could compete with the best sprinters South Africa had produced.

At home, I discovered that my upper gum was badly damaged, my two front teeth loose.

Attacks on American Dudes became so common that we had to walk in groups. Some decided to take the war to the Mapantsulas and beat anyone wearing Mapantsula clothes. It was gang warfare all over again and it soon became clear that thugs had joined the American Dudes to use us as a cover for their nefarious deeds. The movement lost the carnival spirit and became a fully-fledged gang terrorising the community.

# Nkawana is dead

BEFORE I LEFT THE AMERICAN DUDES, I befriended a brooding lanky fellow called Bongani "Nkawana" Gasa. Unlike many of the other Dudes, Bongani was politically astute, an operative intent on sowing seeds of political consciousness and activism among our ranks.

He took me to the first meeting of the Azanian People's Organisation – Azapo. When I joined the organisation in the early 1980s it was the only credible voice espousing black sentiments. Guided by black consciousness principles, Azapo was about self-esteem and self-worth at a time when colonialism and apartheid had brought about feelings of inadequacy and self-loathing among black people.

The fact that many of us robbed and killed members of our communities was evidence enough of this self-loathing. Black consciousness meant to reverse this trend and imbue black people with the willingness and the ability to challenge the status quo and demand their rights.

Nkawana encouraged me to bring more recruits into Azapo. Naturally one of the first few people I turned to was Nhlanhla, the old thug. He was militant enough and read most of the pamphlets and books I passed onto him, but he never joined the organisation. There was a palpable fear in the township at that time as people were arrested for belonging to and furthering the aims of banned organisations such as the ANC. People were also arrested for being in possession of banned literature. Biko's *I Write What I Like* could have landed me in jail, but I managed to distribute this and Azapo magazines at school.

One of these was a classmate, Cebo Nxumalo, who called me "Touch My Blood" because I used to say this when shaking a friend's hand. But as much as he was a fervent believer in the struggle, like Nhlanhla, he was dead scared of getting into trouble with the security police. The state's agents were everywhere, you had to be careful about passing on banned literature.

But Cebo also believed whites had a role to play in the struggle, and regarded black consciousness as exclusivist. What he misunderstood was that no one ever said black consciousness was an end in itself. Black consciousness was a means to a non-racist end.

We argued often until Cebo would shake his head in exasperation, and change the topic. "Touch My Blood, my friend, I am not defending the white man. In fact I admire you for your forthrightness. You are doing a good job of conscientising our schoolmates. Because of people like you, they are beginning to question things. They are beginning to pay more attention to stories in newspapers. But I still maintain that your philosophy is myopic and borders on racism."

I was in standard nine and keen to spread the political message at school. I approached the principal, Mr Shangase, with an idea about starting a newspaper.

My intention was to read a selection of self-generated news stories about the school and township and some general news after the morning prayers. As my class teacher was behind the project, the principal gave me the go-ahead.

The first day I stood on the stage to read a few news items I trembled with nerves. As a member of the debating society, I was a confident public speaker, but I had never addressed such a big crowd without a microphone or a loud-hailer. My voice was squeaky and some of the students laughed. But the next time was easier and there was less laughter, and by the third day I had their rapt attention. Soon pupils brought me snippets of information about youth meetings, music competitions, community meetings, and, hey, the girls were giving me the eye!

One of the teachers who gave me most encouragement was my history teacher, the soft-spoken Mr Gatsha Zondi. He suggested I should follow a career in journalism and also stressed how history had to be rewritten to correct the political bias of colonialism and apartheid. A story of his that I've never forgotten concerns some eight hundred black men who sailed for Europe in January 1917 to fight with the British and allied troops in the First World War. Their vessel was the SS *Mendi*.

Thousands of black South Africans, believing that by expressing loyalty to Britain they would be treated as equals by their white rulers, signed up to fight. They also hoped that afterwards they would be given the vote, given back land rights, and have equal access to jobs and education.

It was, however, explained to these black men that they would not be on active combat in Europe – they would be cooks and cleaners. Despite these ground rules, they enlisted.

The *Mendi* sailed safely to England then headed for Le Havre, France, where the men were to serve. In thick mist some twelve miles off St Catherine's Point on the Isle of Wight, the *Mendi* was struck on the starboard side by the SS *Darro*. She began to list and sink.

In these fraught moments, one of the men, Reverend Isaac Wauchope Dyobha, started dancing. According to Norman Clothier, in his account, *Black Valour: The South African Native Labour Contingent, 1916 – 1918 and the Sinking of the Mendi*, Dyobha admonished his comrades, "Be quiet and calm, my countrymen, for what is taking place is exactly what you came to do. You are going to die . . . but that is exactly what you came to do. Brothers, we are drilling the death drill. I, a Xhosa, say you are my brothers. Swazis, Pondos, Basutos, we die like brothers. We are the sons of Africa. Raise your war cries, brothers, for though they made us leave our assegais in the kraal, our voices are left with our bodies."

Of the eight hundred black troops on board, six hundred and fifteen perished. The *Darro* made no attempt to rescue the survivors who ended up at Dieppe and Arques-la-Bataille where some died and were buried. (Zondi's retelling of the story moved me greatly, and subsequently I have stood among those graves in the black section of the graveyard, saddened that there was only one account of their heroic role.) Zondi also impressed upon me that it was incumbent upon us as young black people to speak up and demand our rightful place in the history of our country.

By climbing onto that stage at school every morning, I had begun my journey towards reclaiming my history.

When my news reading programme was at its zenith, a number of my classmates volunteered as researchers and writers and one even took a stab at reading the news. Buoyed by the success, I took to inserting into each bulletin items that served my own personal political agenda. News about the Azanian Students Movement began to feature frequently.

However, the slant of the news soon irked some pupils who were members of Inkatha. I accepted an Inkatha supporter onto the team and whenever he presented the news it had a strong Inkatha bias. But this was not ideal, and before matters got out of hand I decided to take firm control of the editorial direction. A semblance of balanced reporting was brought in. Newsworthiness became my rallying cry. Of course I cut down on stories that were overtly pro-Azapo and insisted on editing each presenter's script.

One morning I had to read a disturbing story about Bongani "Nkawana" Gasa, the one who'd recruited me into Azapo. He'd gone missing. His distraught family scoured the local mortuary, clinics, nearby police stations and prisons without finding him. A year later I learned that he had joined ANC guerrilla fighters in exile. After a few months' military training he returned to South Africa as part of a group, but they were ambushed by government *askaris* and killed.

# The going gets tough

MY FINAL YEAR OF HIGH SCHOOL, 1984, started quietly enough although many of those who had begun high school with me were no longer part of the class. Some had dropped out and gone to work as labourers in the Hammarsdale industrial area. Others had succumbed to crime and violence. Yet others had fled the country to join the liberation fighters.

Most of my close friends had stayed on in school. Future careers now became an issue. My maths teacher was convinced that I was material for medical school, a sentiment shared by my mother. I was told that as there were good scholarships and bursary schemes for medical students I would not have to worry about funds.

University fees were a major consideration as the financial situation at home had not improved, in fact, it had worsened. My parents' financial responsibilities had increased while their earning capabilities had deteriorated. My father was earning about R250 a month, and his obsession with soccer had exacerbated his already precarious financial situation. As a machinist at a textile factory in Hammarsdale my mother's weekly salary was R28. Even I as a part-time gardener I earned R10 a day. No wonder workers at the factory called it *kwaMdidiwenja* – dog's arse.

Then my mother fell pregnant with her eighth child. The child was named Nokukhanya – "the bringer of light". In times of desperation we attach hope to everything. But in financial terms she was another mouth to feed, another child to rear, another body to clothe, another person in need of space in a four-roomed little house.

Because of our desperate situation my mother had to find another job immediately after giving birth. Thankfully, the skills she had acquired at kwaMdidiwenja landed her a job at the shoe company Bata, where my father was a packer. The salary was better than previously.

But she didn't last long at the new job. She fell seriously ill with hypertension, and her legs and feet troubled her. Because she was no longer strong enough to operate the pedal machine, the company got rid of her.

God intervened. My mother's elder sister, Selina, opened a butchery with money inherited from her late husband. She gave my mother a job, but the pay was low. Meanwhile, my father was having a hard time maintaining such a big family and also subsidising his soccer team. The man I knew as strong-willed, ambitious and focused began to cave in under the financial responsibilities and took to drinking. To make matters worse, Dubazane, his co-manager, also started drinking. This led to a fight with his stepson who stabbed him in the face, blinding him in one eye. The stepson, Babo, ran away from home and Dubazane, too, abandoned his wife and children. A few months later, Babo was killed in a knife fight. His death was blamed on Dubazane. People claimed he had used muti to kill his stepson.

Financially challenged, and now without a friend and a confidant, my father slipped deeper into depression. In the face of all this, my mother and my maths teacher were determined that I go to medical school the following year. On the other hand my English teacher – coincidently my maths teacher's brother – believed this would be a waste of money and time. I was a born writer, he argued, having read some of my early work. He thought my future lay in journalism.

The poems and short stories I showed him earned his praise and encouragement, although they were weak imitations of William Blake and James Hadley Chase.

"You have a lot of writing talent in you," he told me, "but you are still a rough diamond that needs a lot of polishing. You need to be yourself. Write about what you see, about what you know best. Why write about America when you hardly have a grasp of their brand of English? Why not write about gangsters in this township? Why not write about drunks and taxi drivers of the township?"

He urged me to see a man called Mafika Pascal Gwala. Because Gwala was famous – or notorious – I knew who he was. I even knew his house. I couldn't understand how a university-educated teacher could recommend that one of his charges should seek advice from a rabble-rousing drunk who was in and out of jail because of his political beliefs. Gwala was not a member of Azapo. Nor was he involved in any political activities that I was aware of, except for staggering about in the street drunkenly insulting our chief minister, Chief Mangosuthu Buthelezi. I didn't know what class of revolutionary this man was, so one day I decided to find out.

# Mafika, my guru

MAFIKA PASCAL GWALA was either a world-famous poet with an incisive mind, a committed trade unionist and a conscientious political activist from the black consciousness school, or he was a drunk whose gargantuan thirst for booze could only be matched by his larger than life libido.

Before going to his place, I'd done some preliminary research. Many people knew he was highly educated and political. But not many people knew his business. He was so prominent yet so private. Many would observe derisively, "Ag, what's the use of an education if you're going to end up being a layabout drunk who doesn't even hold a job?"

I discovered that Gwala had published two successful and award-winning collections of poetry, *Joliinkomo* and *No More Lullabies*. He had published a number of short stories and essays in both local and international literary journals and anthologies. He had been visited by the legendary Steve Biko. This was the man who was often to be found sitting on a street corner in front of a fire, drinking a gut-corroding concoction called *isqatha* with a group of layabouts.

With a sheaf of short fiction and poetry under my arm, I knocked on his door. The windows were open but there was no response to my knocking. I went round the back to the kitchen. Here, too, the windows were open but the door was closed, I knocked loudly. Again no response. I was about to leave when the door flew open.

"What do you think you are doing? Do you think my bloody doors are for playing?" The man had thick spectacles, a bushy beard and long unkempt hair. I held my breath so as not to inhale his sour breath. "Boy, I'm talking to you! Why are you playing with my doors?"

"Sorry, sir, I wasn't playing. I was knocking."

"If you weren't playing so why didn't you open the door and come in and get your business done and go home and leave me to my business?"

"I couldn't come in because no one said I must come in."

"Well then, what do you want?"

"I wish to speak to Mr Gwala, sir. My teacher sent me to Mr Gwala."

"Who's your teacher?"

"Mr Mungwe, sir."

He thought about it for a while. Then, leaving the door open, he turned his back on me and walked into the house.

I stood at the door, uncertain about my next move.

"Are you going to stand in front of that door forever or are you coming in?"

"Sorry," I said.

The room which was supposed to be a kitchen did not appear to be a conventional place for preparing food and cleaning dishes. There were no cooking utensils for one thing. Instead, books were strewn all over the floor, lying face down, open at strategic places. I had to be careful not to step on them. The place smelt of musty old books, stale beer, stale food, cigarettes, human sweat.

A big rickety table with a typewriter on it occupied a corner. Next to it was a wooden chair that had seen better years. A smaller table was cluttered with a bottle of half-finished beer, a packet of cigarettes and an ashtray overflowing with half-smoked cigarettes. There was also a plate with a partly eaten meal of fish and chips.

"You can finish my food if you are hungry," he said. Adding, "Sit there," he pointed at an upturned beer crate, "and let's hear what Fole Mungwe sent you to get from me. I know I don't owe him because we don't drink together. I am not a teacher anymore. The teacher types don't drink with me anymore."

I handed him my manuscripts and quickly explained that my teacher thought he could help me fix my lines into proper short stories and poems. I told him where I lived, who my parents were, and what career they thought I should follow.

He snatched the pieces of paper from me and browsed through them.

"For the life of my ancestors, why do your teachers tell you that poetry can only be written in archaic English. Thee, thou, thy, thine. What rubbish is this. Is this what Fole teaches you?"

"But Shakespeare writes like that. So does Blake and TS Eliot."

He looked at me. "Have you heard of Soyinka? Oswald Mtshali? Chris van Wyk? Why do you tell me about dead white men?"

"But at school they don't tell us about the people you've just mentioned."

"School doesn't hold all the answers to life; it doesn't hold the answers to literary wisdom. Go to the library and find out."

"But we don't have a library in this township."

"Ah," he grunted, a smirk on his face, "you got me there. But try to find out about South African writers, African poets. Write about what you know."

"I see." I smiled. "That's what my teacher said the other day. My teacher says I must concentrate more on my writing if I want to start my studies in journalism next year."

"Anyway, why do you think you want to write? Other boys like you are playing soccer, chasing skirts and you are wasting your time copying dead white men. Where's your sense of wonder, sense of excitement?"

"I enjoy reading and writing. I want other people to enjoy stories that I dream up, ideas that come to my head . . ."

He burst out laughing. "You know what one Hollywood writer once said? He said if you have something to say, hire a hall; if you want to change the world get yourself a machine gun." He became serious again. "You can write for fun, but don't play with fire. Leave journalism alone. You know what the system is doing to journalists? You know what they've done to Percy Qoboza? [As editor of the *The World* and then *The Post*, Qoboza was in and out of jail for writing anti-government editorials.] What you can do is this: take your parents' advice and study medicine. Be a good doctor and stay out of trouble."

"Biko studied medicine but still couldn't stay out of trouble. The system finds you no matter where you're hiding."

He looked at me for a long time. Then sniggered quietly – te-he-he, te-he-he. The snigger became a loud, throaty guffaw. "I, hah hah hah,

I, hah hah hah, I think I'm going to like you kid. I really do." Taking his glasses off and wiping his eyes, he recovered from the fit of laughter, and said, "Now I want to finish what I was writing."

He ducked under the table and emerged clutching a bundle of magazines. The title of the magazine was *Staffrider*.

"Take these home and read them thoroughly. When you come back here next Friday, I expect you to have written two things: a short story about Doris, and a poem about your neighbour Sis May."

Doris was a guy (I don't know why he had a girl's name) who washed taxis at the rank. Sis May ran a shebeen from her house.

Write about what you know.

# An accidental ringleader

ABOUT TWO WEEKS AFTER my encounter with Mafika Pascal Gwala, my maths teacher, Ma'am Zwane, was transferred to a school in a neighbouring township. The Circuit Office that determined the placement of teachers gave no explanation nor provided another teacher. A delegation of boys from the matric class lodged a plea with the principal to have her brought back. The principal said he couldn't go against a government decision.

In my morning news bulletin the following day, I reported on the incident only to be hauled into the principal's office and accused of inciting lawlessness and unrest. I was warned to retract my news item the following day.

Early the following morning I gathered a few trusted friends and told them that I would not be reading the news. Moreover, I said, we had to take our grievance to the Circuit Office ourselves.

When the first bell rang, summoning us to the assembly square, we were still arguing about taking the matter into our own hands. What if the Circuit Office set the riot police on us? Were we prepared to be locked up for causing a "public disturbance", to use the government's language?

At the end of assembly we rejoined our classes. As the teachers knew about our meeting they stayed in the staffroom which gave us an opportunity to discuss the matter with our classmates. The girls, who normally took the cue from us, were decisive: no classes until the maths teacher was reinstated. The battle should be taken to the Circuit Office. Even the more politically conservative boys advocated action. There were cheers and ululations. Before we left, a few of us appealed for sanity and asked that everyone show respect for elders and order. With hastily made placards, we left the classroom shouting, "Forward with people's education, forward!" We were soon joined by other pupils.

The march to the circuit inspector's office was three kilometres and people cheered and encouraged us along the way with shouts of viva! At the office we asked the horde of students to stand outside the gate while a smaller delegation sought an audience with the circuit inspector.

We entered the office and were told rudely by a secretary that the circuit inspector was out of town and would only be back the following day.

We asked to speak to the deputy. We were told he was busy. Our frustration exploded.

"*Hheyi, wentombazana*! Hey, you girl! We have come all the way from kwaNongoma to get an education here. Now you've taken our teacher away from us without telling us. We want an explanation now!"

"If you don't bring some official to address us now," warned my friend Cebo, "we will have no option but to tell those children outside to break the fence down and break these walls."

"And don't you dare phone the police because they will only make things worse," I joined in.

The receptionist huffed away into an adjoining room. A few minutes later she came back accompanied by a short, pot-bellied man with a pudgy face and a bald head.

"Yes," he said, knitting his brow, "what's happening here?"

"Who are you?" I retorted.

The man's eyes widened with disbelief. I looked sideways at my comrades for support. They shuffled their feet.

Sensing an uncertainty the short man pressed ahead, singling me out. "Boy, don't your parents teach you respect? Is that how you're supposed to speak to your elders?"

I had nothing to lose now, I said, "I'm asking you who you are because we said we wanted to speak to the circuit inspector and we were told he is out of town. So who are you?"

"Yes, who are you?" the others chorused.

With sweat beading on his brow, the man said, "I am Mr Sibeko, the deputy circuit inspector."

"Thank you, sir," we said, and laid our complaint. He listened and

125

said, "But you can't just come here and tell us to reverse a decision that's been made by the circuit inspector, by the government . . ."

"With due respect, sir," I said, "all we are asking of your office is respect for our future, respect for our rights. Quarterly exams are just around the corner, yet we do not have a maths teacher."

"But I don't know what to do. The circuit inspector is not here."

"Not a problem, sir, we will come to this office every day until we get an audience with the circuit inspector, until something is done about our maths teacher . . ."

"No, no, no, I'm not fighting with you boys. I mean, I will raise the matter with the circuit inspector. But please go back to your school, go back to your classes before children from other schools join and there's chaos in our streets."

We left with a promise to return the following day.

The next morning we went to assembly as usual. I read my bulletin as usual. We dispersed to our different classes. Pupils were talking excitedly about the bravery and the discipline that had been displayed at the circuit inspector's office.

Many couldn't get over the newsboy's squeaky-voiced confrontation with the deputy circuit inspector. His brazen, "Who are you?"

One lesson that we learned from the march was that the black functionaries of apartheid could destroy the future of black children without thinking. This had to stop. We discussed our next move. But before we could get much further our class teacher, Mr Nkosi, burst into the classroom. He had his sleeves rolled up, a cane in his hand. "Sit down and shut up!" he shouted. He had been absent the previous day and clearly had only just heard of our escapade. "Why do you embarrass me like this? I am your class teacher, but you go over my head and march all the way to the circuit inspector's office? What do you think the circuit inspector is going to think of me, my authority and ability to control my children, huh? Who were the ringleaders? Khumalo, you are the prefect of this class. You are the journalist of the school. Who were the ringleaders?"

"I was one of them, sir," I said, and the others stepped up too.

126

He turned to me. "Khumalo, I thought you were a prefect, a boy eager for a good education. Now I hear you hang around with jailbirds like Mafika Gwala. Communists, drunks. People with no future. You want to go to jail. Do you realise that this township is awash with government spies who will have your name blacklisted? Do you know what that means? Once blacklisted, no school in this country will ever take you! Is that what you want? Is that how you want to thank the Almighty who blessed you with such wonderful brains."

He addressed the class. "All you fools are allowing yourselves to be controlled by these . . . these puppets who are being used and controlled by the terrorists, communists. You want to throw your future into the dustbins?"

He slashed out with his cane. He was almost in tears. As I tried to block the blows, he bellowed, "You're clenching your fists at me. You want us to fight? Let's go outside now. I will not be humiliated by children in front of the Circuit Office, in front of government."

Nkosi didn't realise that he had become a perpetrator of oppression himself. Ordinarily, he was an easy-going man, but when it came to matters of authority, he bowed down while the system pissed on his head. He refused to confront apartheid.

However, a few days later the maths teacher was reinstated. We had triumphed.

# Pick up the spear

BECAUSE OUR TOWNSHIP WAS SMALL and located in the desolate Natal Midlands with limited access to the mass media, the news sometimes eluded us. By the time we woke up to new developments, history would have moved on a chapter. For example, we knew that the United Democratic Front had been formed in 1983, but the full impact of this only hit us the following year.

Shortly before the formation of the UDF, rent boycotts and attacks on government-elected councillors and administrators were spiralling out of control, particularly in Lamontville. Msizi Dube, the man at the centre of the rent boycott there, was murdered, and days later the community – particularly members of the Masibonisane Lamontville Youth Organisation and the Joint Rent Action Committee, front organisations formed by underground operatives of the ANC – went on the rampage. They hunted down and killed members of a gang called *Amashaolin* as it was believed they were behind the murder of Dube. Two members were murdered in quick succession.

The township plunged into chaos. Youngsters burned down the houses of councillors, people associated with councillors were murdered. Inspired and disturbed by this upsurge of violence, Mbongeni Ngema, who would later make a name for himself in the theatrical arts through the movie *Sarafina!*, wrote and directed a play called *Asinamali!* – "we have no money", the slogan of the rent boycott. The play was a systematic attack on government stooges and an acid commentary on the exploitative rent system.

By the time the Natal region of the United Democratic Front was finally launched in May 1983, most townships were on the boil. Inkatha saw the new political player as a threat, believing that they had come to undermine their authority and confuse their members. Street battles flared in a number of townships.

When Ngema brought *Asinamali!* to my township it provoked an Inkatha attack. No sooner had the performance begun, than members of Inkatha, armed with knobkerries and guns, stormed in, beating up members of the cast and the audience. Soon an actor lay dead. By the time I got to the scene there were policemen, black and white, milling around. A senior police officer ordered us to disperse.

Angry youths asked why the police hadn't intervened when Inkatha launched the attack. In response the police charged towards us; we retaliated with a rain of stones and other missiles. But we were no match against their guns and teargas canisters. We ran for our lives.

At about this time the ANC in exile called for the country to be made ungovernable. The cry was taken up with alacrity. Law and order, such as it was, collapsed. Policemen could no longer venture into the townships for fear of being murdered. The people took charge of the running of the townships – reconnecting defaulters who had been cut off from the electricity grid, reconnecting those who had had their water cut off, presiding over trials of criminals.

Much as the fighting was between pro-government forces and a phalanx of anti-government masses, there were also skirmishes between members of the UDF and Azapo. Chaos had been let loose. As I discovered when I attended an Azapo meeting wearing a T-shirt with a picture of the human rights lawyer Griffiths Mxenge, who had been murdered a few years previously. Mxenge was known to have links to the ANC, and most Azapo members regarded the ANC and the UDF as sell-outs because they subscribed to the Freedom Charter's proclamation that South Africa belonged to all who lived in it. Azapo believed the white oppressors shouldn't own any of the country.

"Comrade, this is out of order," I was told. "Why are you wearing a Varara [UDF] T-shirt? Don't you know these people are killing our comrades?"

"Comrade, political tolerance and open-mindedness," I pleaded. "We are all fighting for the same cause but are we so narrow-minded that we are allowing the system to plant seeds of distrust and violence among us."

"Comrades," intervened an older man, "don't fight among yourselves now. We know that the Charterists are killing our people, Inkatha is killing our people, the system is killing our people. But we must keep in mind that both Azapo and the Charterists are on the same side, being attacked by the system which is using Inkatha as cannon fodder. But in any case, we should always remember that the Black Conscious-ness Movement also had a hand in the formation of this UDF thing, although some of their supporters don't know that."

Indeed, various hues and generations of African activism since the Second World War had come together in the UDF – except Azapo. And many in the organisation couldn't understand how I could break bread with the Charterists when they'd rather be breaking their noses.

After this confrontation I went to my guru Mafika Gwala to submit the poem he had said I should write about Doris, the man who washed cars at the taxi rank.

"These arseholes are fiddling while the country burns," Mafika fumed when I told him about the T-shirt incident. "The system is out to get all of us, and they are quibbling over T-shirts. Do they know what Mxenge did for the struggle? Nincompoops like these shouldn't be al-lowed to speak on behalf of Biko. They don't know anything about black consciousness and its essence."

Biko gazed at us from a huge picture on Mafika's wall, smiling as if mocking our stupidity, our impotence.

We were joined by a number of young men and Mafika handed out drinks, saying, "I declare the meeting open. And let me introduce to you our youngest and newest member, Vusi Khumalo."

So I became a member of the Mpumalanga Arts Ensemble, a group of talented painters, poets, short-story writers, critics, amateur mu-sicians. The group was unashamedly pro-UDF, although the talks and the debates were outright black consciousness. In due course I realised that this was the home I had been looking for. A home of artists who had an open-ended forward-looking interpretation and understanding of black consciousness.

The group exposed me to the latest in political theory, while also

circulating books of new poetry, short stories and basic English gram-
mar.

But the political instability shattered our association. Ben Dikobe
Martins, a respected painter and poet who had been on the run from
the police for a long time, was arrested and given a long prison sentence. When he was apprehended, the group scattered – some leaving
the township altogether. Mafika warned me that the cops might question me about him so I left home to live with Thabo Maila, a classmate,
in another part of the township. I was sixteen, turning seventeen in a
few months. Thabo had the house to himself as his parents were living
in Johannesburg. For security reasons he had encouraged four other
friends, among them Cebo Nxumalo, to spend time at his house. We
formed a study group, and the mutual help worked well because we
all improved our results dramatically. By the time the matric exams
arrived we were more than ready.

But shortly before the exams started I travelled to Johannesburg
with other members of the Mpumalanga Arts Ensemble to attend a
writers' symposium. The car was driven by the world-famous photographer Omar Badsha, and the group included Sfiso Mkame who would
later reach international renown as an artist. At the conference I
brushed shoulders with big-name writers and photographers including
Chris van Wyk, Jeremy Cronin and Colin Smuts. The debates revolved
around the need for artists to throw in their lot with the liberation
movement. It was a call to arms, and for a sixteen-year-old to be told
to use his art to advance the struggle was a heady message. I was the
youngest and least politically sophisticated in the gathering. Much flew
over my head but I had a good time nevertheless. Being in the presence of such great talent, such incisive minds was inspiring in itself,
almost unbelievable. I knew that back home my friends would either
refuse to believe me, or wonder what I was on about because most of
them had not discovered the excitement of reading.

We returned from Johannesburg on a Sunday. On the Tuesday I
wrote my first exam paper. Members of my study group were concerned about my irresponsible behaviour in abandoning the study group

and going to Johannesburg without even telling my parents. How could I consort with the likes of Mafika Gwala, a communist and a drunk? They whispered darkly that Khumalo would fail his exams and bring to his door members of the security police.

Fortunately they were wrong. I passed matric. Not only was I the top student in my school, but in all the schools in our township.

To mark the results me and my friend Scelo Masinga were feted by the mayor of the township, Rodger Dinga Sishi.

On the night of the dinner party he promised to pay for my tertiary education and a few days later I applied to the University of Zululand to study towards a degree in communication. I was accepted, and because of my good matric results, the university awarded me a merit bursary.

My parents' happiness and relief at this turn of events was short-lived. Soon political violence escalated, reminding my parents that the previous year five students had been killed by Inkatha on the university campus.

"Knowing that you can't keep your political noises to yourself," my mother said one day, "we don't believe you should go to *Ongoye* [the other name for the university]. They will kill you."

After much agonising, and consultation with the likes of Mafika, I cancelled my application to the university and turned down the merit bursary. I went to the mayor and reminded him about the promise he'd made on the night of the party. He pointed out that I'd been offered a scholarship by the University of Zululand which I'd foolishly turned down. In the light of this, he couldn't help me. I said that the university was a war zone. But he wouldn't listen to me, just as years before he had turned down my father's appeal for sponsorship of his soccer team.

# Drinking from the forbidden well

THE FOLLOWING YEAR, 1985, I was among a horde of students who converged on the Technikon Natal intent on studying journalism. At the
time the technikon was the only institution in the province offering a
diploma in journalism.

After a frantic fund-raising campaign – appealing to neighbours, to
members of my extended family – my parents had raised R1 000 which
enabled me to register. Everyone's generosity in my hour of need made
me feel appreciated, and I vowed to make them proud of my achieve-
ments.

Many of the prospective students were well dressed. They had been
dropped off by parents who drove cars. I had commuted the fifty kilometres by bus, I was dressed in threadbare jeans, T-shirt and sneakers.
But I was still pleased that I had come this far in life. I felt an affinity
with the crowd milling around me. However, I might have been in a
crowd, but I was alone. Most of the students were white.

After queuing for a few hours at the administration office, my turn
finally came. I approached the clerk and told her I could pay for the
tuition fees for the year upfront. I was promptly, if politely, turned
away. The law stated that I had to register at an institution reserved
for "my own people". Unless I had special permission from the Minister of Education, I should apply at ML Sultan, an Indian institution.

As I turned to go, I noticed some white kids staring at me, some of
them sympathetically, others with self-satisfied smirks that said,
serves you right, darkie, don't you know you don't belong here?

Angry, frustrated, insulted and belittled, I arrived at Sultan and told
them I wanted to study journalism. They apologised profusely that although journalism was on their prospectus, they would only be intro-
ducing it the following year. I was then referred to Mangosuthu Technikon, a black institution in Umlazi, a township twenty minutes away

by taxi. I didn't bother to go there because I knew that Mangosuthu didn't offer journalism.

It was not out of naivety that I had gone to Technikon Natal. I knew that the institution had produced excellent journalists, both black and white, but I also knew that it was, by law, still a white institution. A black person had to beg, cajole, threaten and fight for a place. I had excellent matric grades and I had the money, I decided to fight. I was not going to back down and register for a teacher's diploma at the local college like most of my classmates.

I trudged back to the technikon. The clerk who had turned me away was still there. I explained to her that I had been to both ML Sultan and Mangosuthu and that neither institution offered journalism.

"I am afraid I can't help you," she said impatiently, "why don't you choose something else from Sultan – management, engineering – they've got a lot of things to offer."

"But I want to study journalism, and I've got my full tuition fees with me."

"I'm afraid our journalism school is full now," she said.

"But I know that's not true!"

A big-chested white man with bushy eyebrows approached us at a furious pace. As a seasoned stone-thrower who was no stranger to angry white men in uniforms, I thought that I was in trouble for having raised my voice. But to my surprise, the man turned on the clerk: "What did you just tell him? Don't you realise he has a right to register with us if no one else is offering what he wants to study?"

The man ordered the clerk to help me fill in the forms. I felt like pulling faces at her, as kids do when they've been vindicated. The bushy-eyebrowed man turned out to be Clive Emdon, the head of the journalism department. Over the years, he'd helped many black students enter the programme or access bursaries.

Having registered, I now faced another problem: accommodation. Black people were not allowed to stay on campus, and finding accommodation elsewhere in town was in itself another test. For one thing there was the Group Areas Act which put the "white residential area" beyond bounds, although I knew some black students squatted in white suburbs. Those who could afford to would ask a white person to act as a proxy renter of a flat in town. But that meant creeping around surreptitiously, pretending to be a cleaner or a messenger, having to use the staircase rather than the lift, and always on the alert for the supervisor. Should the police be called, you'd be back on the streets. But a proxy flat wasn't an option as I couldn't afford to pay the rent anyhow.

For the first few weeks, I commuted daily. This further drained our financial resources, and it meant leaving before sunrise. In the afternoons I couldn't spend as much time as I would have liked at the library because the last bus left at 5 p.m. By the time I got home I was tired, but as there was no room to work until everyone had gone to bed, this meant late nights by candlelight.

Life in class was stressful. Out of fifty students, there were seven Africans, three Indians and the rest were white. But that was not the cause of the stress. English being the second or third language for the black students, we had to work harder than our white classmates. Never before had we interacted with whites from a position of supposed equality. Whereas the white people I had gardened for enunciated each and every word In. Order. To. Be. Sure. The boy. Under-stood. What. It was. He was. Required. To do. Now these people were talking through their noses in their sing-song accents so fast I couldn't-understand-what-it-was-they-were-talking-about-that-was-supposed-to-have-happened-during-the-French-Revolution-in-France.

Nevertheless, I worked hard at my books, at my listening skills, at my pronunciation. Writing was never much of a problem.

Whenever they find themselves in the minority, blacks tend to gravitate together even if, under normal circumstances, they wouldn't have acknowledged one another's existence. This is what happened in our class. From the way we dressed, spoke and carried ourselves, it was clear that we were a disparate bunch socially. For example, in two instances my peers' mothers were nurses, another's was a domestic servant, while Gugu Kunene's father was the famous Obed Kunene, editor of *Ilanga* newspaper. Together with the Indian students we got along well as a group, sharing a vague political camaraderie.

The interloper was a stout white fellow called Fred Kockott. While some of the white guys played at being politically radical, Fred was just a humble guy trying to understand his strange homeland. He had grown up without an opportunity to understand black people and their languages, let alone that they could love, hate, dream, bleed, be pissed off, cry and smash up things and themselves just like white people.

Most whites I knew carried their whiteness as if it were dynamite, ready to use it to hurt other people. Fred Kockott wore his whiteness like an elegant suit that does not call attention to itself, but could be appreciated by those who understood fashion. Fred was white, but he couldn't help it.

One day, Fred invited me for a drink. My knowledge of campus was limited: I would walk in the gate, go to class, go to the cafeteria (if I had money), go to the library, and then go home. I didn't know there was a pub. At first I thought Fred was joking. A pub at school? These white people were strange. You tell your parents that you're going to study at technikon, and then you end up drinking alcohol! With the approval of the technikon authorities! My ancestors were right when they said it would take the black man a long time to understand the white man and his ways.

I told Fred no, sorry, I don't drink alcohol. Besides, if I stayed too long, I would miss my bus. He said, not to worry, he'd got a car. So we ended up at a place called Chris' Cave Bar. Never before had I finished a whole bottle of beer by myself. We were soon deep into a racial discussion.

"My problem with you white people is you hate black people yet you don't know them," I said. "How can you hate that which you don't know, which you don't understand?"

"Precisely," he said. "It's the fear of the unknown. We don't understand you, we don't know you. We are, in fact, scared to find out who you really are. We are scared to find out what black people are thinking, that's why the white government has declared a lot of black leaders unquotable in our newspapers. We don't want to know."

"The ostrich syndrome."

"Uh-hum!" He gulped his beer, lit a cigarette, and continued, "It amazes a lot of white people, in case you didn't know, that after all we've done to you, you still haven't murdered us in our sleep. You cook for us, wash for us, nurse our babies, but I have yet to see you guys mounting a national campaign to poison us."

"You're planting ideas in my head now," I said, and we laughed.

Later, we staggered out of the bar. I spent the night on the floor of one of the dormitories. The following morning the word was out that a black person had spent the night at the white hostel.

Over the next few weeks I continued to commute to the technikon, but it was becoming increasingly untenable.

My aunt Theresa heard of my plight. She was now employed by a small operation that made pottery. After hours, she cleaned a house occupied by a melange of hippies and semi-outlaws. In exchange, they allowed her to occupy an outbuilding. She suggested I share this room with her.

# The house on the hill

MY AUNT'S QUARTERS were in Morningside, a wealthy suburb with a sweeping view of Durban's majestic colonial buildings: the shiny skyscrapers, the elegant spires and domes of the churches and mosques.

"A lot of black people – mainly students – are now living in the suburbs," my aunt told me as we walked leisurely up Berea Road. "They do so illegally of course, because the Group Areas Act is still in force."

"What happens if the police catch you in a building designated for white occupation?" I asked. "Do they still arrest you and send you back to black South Africa like they used to do in the old days?"

"They are not as tough as they used to be. There are just too many black people breaking the law, it is now impossible to enforce some of these ridiculous laws. Many black people who stay in the suburb pretend to be working there – as janitors, cleaners, garden boys, and so on. You must learn to blend with these creative types who don't walk so tall as to challenge the white man. Be meek, and you shall survive in white suburbia."

I listened. I didn't think it would be difficult to survive because, as a garden boy, I had learned to play the meek Jim-comes-to-the-big-city type whenever I encountered a white person who wanted to put me in "my place".

We stopped at a corner café to buy a loaf of bread, two pieces of fried fish, chips and a bottle of Coke. The streets were quiet, with only an occasional glimpse of a "kitchen maid" in full uniform, or a "garden boy" sweating behind the white man's shrubbery. The walk from the technikon took half an hour.

The address was 154 Sydenham Road, the house an old double storey set on a large piece of ground. At the back of the main house was a compound in which my aunt and others had rooms. The house belonged to the owner of the pottery factory.

"Welcome to your new home," my aunt said as she opened the door to her room.

Even in the brightness of mid-afternoon the room was completely dark. She fumbled for the light switch. I saw a room about three square metres with no window. The air was heavy with the suffocating torpor of mildew, a green moss smudged the walls. The only piece of furniture was a three-quarter bed. An old beer crate served as a bedside table on which my aunt had her toothpaste, toothbrush, deodorant and a box of matches. Beside this makeshift table was a two-plate electric burner, on it a pot, a couple of coffee mugs and four porcelain plates.

My aunt sat heavily on her bed, sighing with relief.

"Are you going to keep standing there, or are you going to sit down?" she said irritably. "What are you staring at? I never promised you it was going to be heaven. It's just a shelter for us to hide our heads under. Grab a plate, sit down and let's eat and go to sleep. There's yet another long day ahead of us tomorrow."

I mumbled an apology, put my bag on the floor and reached for the plates onto which I emptied the packets of fish and chips. I sat on a chair behind the door. We ate in silence.

"Do you now see when we older people keep telling you to work hard with your studies? Do you see?" said my aunt. "Do you think this is the right place for a human being to live? An educated person can afford her own house, flat and car in a decent building. Not your aunt, because she ran away from school. Work hard with your studies – with a little bit of perseverance you will finish your studies. And the way things are progressing now, I think by the time you graduate, this country would have changed. Apartheid is on its way out. People with your intellect and education will be able to live wherever they please, as long as they can pay for the privilege. Look, I am old now. In my early forties. I don't have a place of my own. I don't have a husband. I have nothing. I have three children who can't live with me because I have no place I can call my own. Do you think I like what I am?"

This was an uncharacteristically serious speech from my fun-loving aunt whose conversations were usually about fashion and music.

After we'd eaten, I cleaned up then stood outside while my aunt changed into her sleeping clothes. By the time I came back, she was tucked up. My bedding was a flimsy sponge and two blankets. It reminded me of my early childhood in the crowded house at Chesterville. I made myself comfortable and opened a book. My aunt was already snoring. A few hours later she awoke with a start.

"Why is the light still on? Why is the light still on?" she cried out. "The white people in the main house are going to complain and say I'm eating their electricity. Switch off now!"

I did as she wanted and lay staring into the darkness. Why was my reading always frustrated? My mother had made me douse the candles because she couldn't afford to buy more. Again I was being frustrated. My rage wasn't against my aunt, but against my fate. Would I ever know happiness? Would I ever have peace of mind?

Early the next morning I was woken by a racket outside, excited voices, whistling, snatches of songs.

"Go out and wash, and get ready for technikon," my aunt said from her bed.

"Where is the bathroom?"

"Just follow the voices. You will see other young men like you washing out there. They will know who you are because I forewarned them."

I wrapped a towel around my waist and tiptoed out. Three boys about my age were washing at a big sink. They greeted me by my clan name and invited me to join them. The three were happy although I couldn't understand why. The water was freezing, there was no privacy, the women who lived in the yard could see us in our nakedness, washing at the sink.

After a few days, I got used to the bizarre morning encounters with the brothers at the freezing sink. As I had guessed, they were from some distant rural settlement. And like my dad in his youth, they were happy to be accepted into the periphery of the white man's world. Their papers were in order, they would brag to newcomers from the rural areas. They'd never been to school and didn't realise that one day they would be in a position similar to my aunt, owning nothing, facing a gloomy future. One of them asked why a healthy, able-bodied young man like me was wasting time at school. I should be working, earning money, starting a family.

My explanation puzzled him.

"The laziness of city boys never ceases to amaze me!" he said, shaking his head. "You should be getting a woman to relieve your mother. The old lady must be tired of washing your clothes. You must be saving money to buy cattle for your father's kraal." The brothers and I were Zulus, experiencing the same levels of deprivation, yet we lived in two completely different worlds.

The advantage of my new accommodation was that I could stay at the library until closing time, about nine at night. I wolfed down Tom Wolfe, devoured Friedrich Nietzsche, and allowed the witty, hard-drinking Can Themba to take me into the heart of Sophiatown. My heart and spirit soared with a new confidence, and I sang with Leopold Senghor, through whose poetry I was beginning to see myself.

A few months on my aunt and I started arguing about my failure to contribute money towards the groceries. She knew that I wasn't getting maintenance or pocket money from my parents.

"What about the money you earn from your piece jobs at the white people's gardens?"

"I have to buy books."

"A schoolchild buys books only once a year, at the beginning of each year."

"My parents didn't have money to pay for my books at the beginning of the year. As it is, I am playing catch up, buying books which I should have been provided with at the beginning of the year. Besides, in order to increase my knowledge, I need to buy other books that are not necessarily required by the school. Books are important to me."

"Is that why you are always smelling of alcohol? You think I am stupid? Who are you trying to fool?"

It was true that I was enjoying the odd drink. But I wasn't using my own money. There were many white boys willing to buy a darkie a drink as long as the darkie was prepared to be an anthropological subject.

"How did you make it to technikon in the face of the poverty in the townships? Are your parents teachers or do they work at the bank that they can afford to pay your tuition fees? How does it feel being in the same class as white people? How do you manage to absorb what's being said when you've only started speaking English recently?" I would put up with this for the odd beer or two.

But after a hurtful argument with my aunt, I decided to give her something towards the upkeep of our room.

The gloominess of our room reminded me of conditions Emile Zola described in his novel *Germinal*. One of the stories about Zola had it that in the mines at Anzin he'd encountered an enormous workhorse pulling a sled piled with coal. Zola wanted to know how such a big horse got in and out of the mine every day. Initially the miners thought the great Zola was joking. But when they realised that he was serious, they explained that the horse came down as a small colt and never went back to the surface. Over time, and deprived light, the horse became blind. Here it worked until it died. Here it was buried.

I realised that my own aunt – or any black labourer for that matter – was Zola's horse.

She came into the white world to work, still young strong and energetic. She laboured hard, the white world sapping her strength until she couldn't handle it anymore. The room in which we stayed was an accurate metaphor for the plight of the black worker. Even though I had made friends at the technikon, not one of them knew the conditions under which I lived. Even my black classmates had not been inside the room. I had never been so ashamed in my life. The very location of the dingy mildew-covered room at the extreme end of the property was eloquent enough.

After a few months I met the people who stayed in the main house. One of them was Mike Smith, a relatively well-known rock guitarist. He had played with a singer called Steve Fataar, who in the 1970s was the leader of the Flames, a famous rock band. I met him when he came to visit one day and we sat chatting, enjoying a beer and a spliff. Another famous resident was Dan Kapuejah, a reggae singer. Both Mike and Dan were black men who had "crossed the Rubicon" and had white women as partners. Essentially, they were breaking two laws – the Group Areas Act and the Immorality Act. With a smile in my heart I realised that this was, after all, the right place to be if I was to learn how to break the white man's law.

# A state of emergency

THOSE OF US BREAKING the Immorality Act and the Group Areas Act shouldn't have bothered about being found out. The white man had bigger fish to fry. By 1985 the country was in turmoil.

A shopping centre in the white suburb of Amanzimtoti was ripped apart by a bomb. Several white people were killed. A nineteen-year-old boy from Kwamashu, on the north coast, was subsequently arrested. Andrew Zondo told the court he had been trained by the ANC in guerrilla warfare. He said he had no remorse for this blow against the system, although he regretted the fact that innocent civilians had died. He said he had suffered enough and couldn't take it anymore. This inspired more attacks by youths on government installations, such as police stations, council chambers, schools.

Inevitably, street skirmishes between black citizens and the police became frequent. On March 21, people from Langa township in Cape Town walking to commemorate the famous Sharpeville massacre of 1961 were stopped by police. A heated exchange led to a confrontation that left seventeen people dead. The previous month at least a hundred members of the UDF had been arrested, accused of terrorism. All over the country young people were disappearing, either into jails from which many never came out, or into exile to join ANC or PAC guerrilla fighters.

On July 20, two events gripped the country: a young black woman, Maki Skhosana, was shown on TV being kicked and stoned by an angry mob. They then placed a car tyre round her neck, poured in petrol and set her alight. Rumour had it that she was a police spy who had betrayed six youths who subsequently died at the hands of the police.

On the same day, government declared a state of emergency. This gave police new powers to detain indefinitely and without trial anyone suspected of being a threat to the state. Meetings were banned.

While the state of emergency was meant to calm the country, especially the townships, it had the opposite effect: places which otherwise would have remained unscathed began to feel the heat. My classmate Ricky Naidoo disappeared. We learned that he had been detained. Black students commuting from the townships missed classes because the violence disrupted transport. Besides, a number of youths calling themselves the Comrades were attacking children going to school. Their slogan was: liberation before education. Some upright citizens, in turn, attacked these youths. The vigilante groups became the A Team or the Witdoeke who soon became a law unto themselves, killing those who wouldn't join their anti-Comrades campaigns. The apartheid government saw an opportunity here. It infiltrated and armed these vigilante groups to decimate the young radicals.

Over the next few weeks I visited various townships with friends, either to check on comrades or find new hideouts for those on the run from the police. By June, of the seven black students in my class only two of us remained.

Then on August 5, a day after I celebrated my nineteenth birthday, Victoria Mxenge was murdered. (Years later it would emerge that Mxenge had been murdered by askaris.) Five days later I decided to visit my parents. In the taxi to Mpumalanga the talk ranged from politics to soccer to the weather until someone mentioned that there were rumours that our township was under threat.

"Threat from where, from what?"

"Don't you know? It is said our township is too conservative, that it is the breeding ground of Inkatha."

"What's wrong with being a member of Inkatha?"

"Don't you know it is said Inkatha is the tool of the white man, it is being used by the white government to suppress black anger."

"So who's going to attack the township?"

"Don't say you heard it from me." The man lowered his voice. "It is said that these children who call themselves Comrades, the children of the UDF, are going to attack our township so we can all wake up and dump Inkatha."

Voices were raised. Someone said, "Ag, that's nonsense. If they want to say something to Inkatha, why don't they arrange a meeting with Inkatha? Most of us aren't interested in politics, let me assure you, and we'd rather be left out of all this nonsense."

Somebody else ventured, "Ah, this is just an empty rumour. Do you think our children are crazy enough to start such nonsense?"

"But haven't you been watching television? Didn't you see those children kicking that woman to death and setting her alight? Haven't you read of these Comrades stopping people from going to work? Haven't you heard of them forcing old women to drink cooking oil simply because the ignorant women had bought their groceries from a store which had been earmarked for a consumer boycott? Haven't you read of them burning down schools and shouting 'liberation before education'?"

"Ag, that kind of nonsense only happens in Johannesburg. We Zulus know our children. Our children learn respect and discipline from the minute they are born."

The taxi drove on, the undulating hills of our lovely province rolling steadily past. Cattle and sheep grazed in the veld. In the distance, at the top of a hill, a white farmer's house overlooked the large tract of land he called home.

At the entrance to the township we were stopped by a roadblock. This was unusual. Two tents had been pitched at the side of the road. This was also unusual. Men wearing Inkatha colours and armed with spears, knobkerries and an assortment of other weapons, ushered us out of the taxi. They were courteous, almost jovial.

"Good people," they said, "sorry to disturb your journey. We have to search every car for weapons. These UDF people have threatened to smuggle themselves into our township and start wreaking havoc. We have to make sure they do not get in. We can't surrender our township to the ravages of political nonsense."

Satisfied that we carried no arms, petrol bombs or other weapons commonly associated with the UDF, the self-appointed road marshals waved us on.

Back in the taxi, the passengers were animated.

"You see, I told you. I was not lying when I said those things about the UDF. The UDF is definitely on its way into the township."

"Ag, these people are overreacting. No UDF is going to come and wreak havoc here."

The man who had raised the scare said he was going to a community meeting about this threat to our township.

The taxi dropped me and I rushed home, dropped my bag and left the house immediately. I had my notebook and pen. The community meeting was to be addressed by the mayor, Sishi, and Zakhele Nkehli, the local leader of Inkatha. Nkehli was an ambitious young leader eager to make his mark on the political landscape. Some said he had his eyes on the mayor's seat.

# Nkehli

"War is a time when defeatists are punished and deserters are shot. The tyrant is at war against his own people and his message, endlessly repeated, is that the enemy within will be rooted out."
CHRISTOPHER HOPE, *Brothers Under The Skin*

THE MEETING was held in the Phezulu High School hall, the same place I had once read out the morning news. By the time I arrived there was a throng of people in front of the hall. Some stood in knots of three, four, talking and laughing heartily. Some were dressed in the Inkatha garb of khaki suits, black berets and ties or badges in the organisation's colours: black, green and gold. Men chanted or sang war songs, played with their knobkerries and fighting sticks. This was usual. A self-respecting Zulu man was expected to always carry these traditional accoutrements, especially when going to a meeting or attending an important cultural ceremony.

I spotted the mayor locked in conversation with some well dressed, well girthed people who appeared to be businessmen or councillors. He beckoned me over.

"How big you've grown, young man!" he said, shaking my hand warmly. He turned to his friends and said, "This boy here is going to make us proud one of these days. He is training to be a journalist. He will be the first qualified journalist in our township."

His friends smiled at me, nodded their heads a few times, saying good, good, good, very good.

The mayor continued smugly, "Men of the area, it really gives me a sense of personal triumph when I see our young men progress so." These sentiments from the man who reneged on his promise to pay my tuition fees. "I do sincerely believe that I have contributed by setting an example, by showing these youngsters just what you can accomplish through sheer hard work, perseverance and focus, focus, focus."

"Perseverance, hard work, Mr Mayor, hard work," the sycophants chorused.

The meeting started. The master of ceremonies outlined the programme and introduced the main speaker, councillor Zakhele Nkehli. The mayor and his rotund friends were also seated on the stage.

Nkehli was probably in his mid-twenties, a final-year student at Technikon Natal. His eldest brother was an Inkatha torchbearer and also held a senior position in the legislature of the KwaZulu homeland government.

I had never met Nkehli, although he had once dated a girl I fancied but was too scared to approach. She and I were in the church choir, and after singing practice Nkehli would arrive in his car to fetch her, driving me nuts with jealousy. As it happened, I stayed with the church choir until I finished high school. There was a lingering hope that one day the girl would see the folly of her ways and dump Nkehli so I could move in. She never did.

Nkehli was a rising star in the firmament of young, ambitious Inkatha politicians, trusted, it was said, by Buthelezi.

At a number of council meetings he had undermined the mayor, clearly showing that he wanted to usurp the mayorship. Like a shark he was drawn to blood. Like a shark he only moved forward.

Yet Nkehli's voice couldn't have been smaller or squeakier. I almost laughed when he started chanting Inkatha slogans, his voice high-pitched and trailing off to a strangled cry,

"Inkaaathaa!"

The crowd, punching the air with their fists, responded with a throaty, "Yesizweee!"

"Sonqobaaa!"

"Simunye!"

"Ngoba izwe . . .!"

"Elethu!"

"UShenge!"

"Owethu!"

He then asked the now excited people to be good Zulus and take their seats, "Ayihlale phansi ibamb'umthetho!"

149

"*Seng'hleli!*" the people said as they sat down.

"The reason we have called this meeting, as the mayor here will agree with me, is because we are concerned with what is happening all around us. The country is in flames. Our people are being killed. Their homes are being burned down. Their children are being prevented from going to school. Those who defy the call by the radicals are being attacked left, right and centre."

People shook their heads, and uhmed and aahhed at the mention of these deprecations being visited upon innocent citizens.

"In the face of all this, people of God, what should we do?"

"Action! Action!" some people shouted.

"People of God, we must think before we act. People, we must do what?"

"We must think!"

"Before we do what?"

"Before we act."

"Good. Your good leadership has been thinking on your behalf, people of God. This Inkatha which brought me here in front of you has been doing a lot of thinking on your behalf. People, we thought and thought and looked around. Then we realised that the safety of this very township, this very community, is under threat. Your families, your wives, your husbands, your children are not safe anymore. Whether they are in the street, at school, at work, inside their own homes, they are not safe. The UDF people from Lamontville and Chesterville have let it be known that they are coming to turn this township upside down. They say they want to uproot Inkatha. Now I say, let us see them do that. What do I say?"

"Let us see them do that!"

"My people, all I am saying is that we are ready for the UDF. Our soldiers are manning roadblocks at all entrances to the township. We are searching all incoming cars for suspicious-looking characters and for weapons. I am now convinced that we've done a good job of it. We have managed to keep the UDF people out of the township. But I have a fear. And when a leader like me, when a soldier like me has a fear then you must know that the danger is big. What I am saying, my people, is that while we are busy blocking the UDF from infiltrating our township, there already exist within this very township a couple of nests which are hatching UDF snakes. We must eliminate these nests, hit these snakes on the head."

The crowd buzzed with excitement, clicking and clucking their tongues in anger.

"One of these snakes is with us in this hall."

A huge gasp.

"I said one of these snakes is with us here and now. This snake is that Khumalo boy." He pointed at me. "He has been taking notes ever since I started talking. He thinks we don't know who he is. Of course we know who he is. They keep running around saying Inkatha people are uneducated barbarians who don't understand things. Some of us are very educated and clever. We know that this Khumalo boy is a UDF snake. And what do you do to a snake? You hit its head before it plunges its venomous fangs into your exposed heel. That's what you do to a snake. This Khumalo boy is here to be the ear of the enemy, he is going to give the information to his commanders within the UDF."

There were rumbles of anger from the hall. I tried to get up, to protest my innocence, to point out that Mr Nkehli himself knew that I was a student journalist, that I was a student at the very institution that had made him such an educated and eloquent man. I had my student card on me. But no one was interested. I was grabbed by a group of men.

I shouted at the mayor to come to my rescue, "Baba Sishi, Baba Sishi!"

But the mayor averted his eyes. Outside the hall, one of the men punched my nose. Another spat in my face. I was pushed into the back of a waiting van, blood flowing freely from my nostrils. Inside the van were men armed with gleaming spears. The van drove off, the armed men hitting and punching me.

By the time we arrived at the local police station my face was sore and swollen.

# We are watching you!

IT WAS ONLY AT THE POLICE STATION that I began to ask myself a number of questions: why were the Inkatha people driving around in a police van, armed with spears?

What authority did they have to pick me up from the township – with no charges levelled against me – and bring me to a police station? It had indeed been whispered many times before that Inkatha was a surrogate of the apartheid state, but I had never thought that the collaboration would be so blatant.

When we got to the police station I was roughly kicked out of the van and marshalled to one of the tiny offices inside the police station. By that time I had decided to keep my mouth shut because every utterance I made was rewarded with violence. I was kept standing inside a tiny office with a desk, a filing cabinet, two chairs, a typewriter. There was no one in the office with me. I could hear voices from adjoining offices. At one stage I was tempted to sneak out of the office and run for it. After all, the front part of the police station was busy with people walking in and out. I would hardly stand out as I negotiated my way through the throngs towards the main entrance. The voice of cowardice prevailed, and I kept standing inside that tiny office.

About an hour later the men came back accompanied by a white police official. I could not tell the rank, but he was quite senior with an array of decorations displayed on his chest.

"Why are you causing trouble in my town?" the senior policeman asked in a soft voice.

"Sir, I didn't do anything. I . . ."

*Smack!*

The impact of his hand across my face was like bashing one's face against a wall. I collapsed on the floor, overturning the chair that had been standing innocently next to the desk.

I didn't feel any shame when I realised that I had wet my pants. I got to my feet.

"Look, my boy, you're too young to go around involving yourself in things you don't understand," he said in a tone that could have come from a father worried about a wayward son. "You see what's happening in Soweto and places like that? You see what's happening in Lamontville and Chesterville? Do you want to be used by the terrorists to bring that kind of nonsense into this township?"

"But I haven't done anything . . ."

*Smack!*

This time the blow came not from the white policeman, but from one of the other men who added a rejoinder to the blow, "You must keep quiet when the white man is talking!"

"Take him out of my station!" the white policeman said.

The men looked at each other uncomprehendingly, and looked at the white man as if to say: what do we do with him now?

"I said take him out! Do whatever you want with him, but don't do anything you will regret."

"But Councillor Nkehli said . . ."

"I said *out!*"

I was hauled out of the police station and bundled back into the van. New fears clouded my mind. While I was in the police station I had resigned myself to joining the hundreds of young people who had gone into political detention. Now I wasn't sure what was going to happen to me.

It was late at night when we drove out of the police station. Our first port of call was at the roadblock the Inkatha people had set up at the entrance of the township. Here I was hauled out of the van and paraded before ululating women who were recommending a severe sentence for me because I was one of the troublesome Comrades. Imagine a disciplined member of Azapo being mistaken for a Comrade, a political thug who preached liberation before education, and burned people's houses simply because they held different political views! This was the height of insolence.

One of the women stepped out of the crowd and spat in my face. It was then that I saw Zakhele Nkehli. I shouted at the top of my voice, wanting to know what I had done to him, crying out that whatever I had done to him must be forgiven, and I would leave the township immediately. He gave me a grin and a slight shake of the head before he walked out of the tent where I was detained.

The next face that I recognised almost gave me a heart attack. It was the face of Nyoni Hlongwane, the boy who had tried to intervene on my behalf when I was being attacked by thugs who hated my alliance with the American Dudes. Our eyes met briefly under the bright illumination of the gas lamps.

"Nyoni, brother, please talk to these people, ask them to release me. They are making a mistake. I am not a UDF person. I haven't caused any trouble. You know I am a cool guy who doesn't bother anyone around here. Please." Nyoni looked ashamed and walked away from me. How Nyoni had changed.

A few minutes later, I was made to lie on the ground and some people took turns sjambokking me. Many of those who were asked to sjambok me did it almost reluctantly. I could sense that a lot of them were opposed to the beating I was being given.

Unbeknown to me, elsewhere in the township, Azapo members Strini Moodley and Selby Baqwa had been caught at a roadblock by Inkatha and were being interrogated. Unlike me, they were not beaten, but they were held for several hours while Nkehli interrogated them. I later learned that they were released only on instructions from the Pietermaritzburg security police. Moodley was a journalist and veteran political activist who had been released from Robben Island recently. Baqwa was a prominent human rights lawyer destined to become an advocate. (Ironically, a few years later Baqwa appeared as the defence advocate for a bunch of Inkatha thugs – including one David Marshall Khambule who was a neighbour of mine – who, accompanied by white policemen, had murdered eleven people. The youngest of the victims was a four-year-old boy and the eldest a woman of sixty-six. The attack came to be known as the Trust Feed massacre.)

After the beating my captors bundled me into the van again and drove around the township for a while. Later – it could have been midnight – they dumped me in the middle of nowhere.

"Run!" they told me as I walked hesitantly into the night. "Run! We are watching you!"

I expected them to start shooting at me as I'd seen it done in the movies. But they kept shouting, "Run! We are watching you."

# An indecent proposal

EIGHT DAYS AFTER my hellish experience at the hands of Inkatha, Mandla Mthembu, the executive member of Azapo who had castigated me for wearing a Griffiths Mxenge T-shirt at an Azapo meeting, was attacked. Masked men stabbed him in the back with an assegai while attempting to abduct him from his home. At first his assailants were thought to be UDF members as there was open conflict between Azapo and the UDF elsewhere in the country. But in the following months all doubts as to the attackers would be removed.

In quick succession senior members of Azapo were assaulted, and in each instance they recognised their attackers as known members of Inkatha. When Nkehli was challenged on this he at first disassociated his organisation but then admitted that they were behind the attacks.

Over the next few weeks we debated a plan of action. The older members appealed for discipline, the younger felt that we should fight back. But we had no arms. UDF members in the township – the organisation had established a strong presence and was prepared to stand up to Inkatha – were approached for assistance. They needed to clear the matter with their leadership but conceded that if the attacks persisted this would be taken as a declaration of war and Azapo and the UDF would fight side by side against Inkatha.

The attacks continued. Houses belonging to Azapo leaders were burned down. But the leadership took no action. Instead, high-ranking members fled the township. Inkatha dominated the public space once again, even disrupting meetings of the local textile union which was affiliated to the UDF. The leadership's decision not to fight back angered many of us. Young members started breaking away to join other bodies such as the newly-formed Hammarsdale Youth Congress, an affiliate of the UDF.

Although I didn't join this group, I refused to renew my membership of Azapo. I was pissed off. My sympathies lay with the organisation but I had lost interest in its internal dynamics.

I was also missing classes, using the state of emergency and the attendant street violence as an excuse. Instead I spent time with UDF people being shown how to make petrol bombs and handle small arms. There was also advanced training available for the handling of AK47s, R1s and .303s.

In the midst of this, three of us caught and beat up a junior member of Inkatha, none other than the future killer, David Marshall Khambule.

When two old men tried to intervene, Khambule got away.

"Why are your trying to kill this boy?" the men wanted to know.

"He is Inkatha," we responded.

"You are going to bring us trouble, you kids," one of the old men said. "The Inkatha people will come to this area and attack everyone they see in this street. My boys, please, don't bring us bloodshed."

A few days later – it was a Sunday – I was sitting in our lounge reading a magazine when there was a knock on the door. Still holding the magazine, I opened the door: Zakhele Nkehli stood smiling, flanked by two trusted lieutenants.

"Can we come in, please," he said, still smiling.

"Sure, sure." I tried to hide my shock and fear.

"Is your father around?"

My father had heard the voices and come through to the lounge. The sight of Nkehli jolted him, but he soon regained his composure.

After exchanging polite greetings, Nkehli got down to business. "Baba Khumalo, we come here in peace. You will recall that not so long ago there was a misunderstanding between my people and your boy here. I have no grudge against him, and I hope the feeling is mutual. You have a clever intelligent boy in Vusi, I must congratulate you, Baba Khumalo. This is exactly why we are here. We are here to explore ways of how we can channel his intellect and energy. He has a lot to contribute to this community."

"I don't think I am following you," replied my father, glancing at me.

"Vusi here can speak for himself, if he understands what you want from him. What is it that you want exactly?"

"To cut a long story short, Baba Khumalo, we need to enlist your son's services as one of our organisers. He has the education, the intellect and the connections. People will listen to him. We need him to join Inkatha, and leave his wayward experiments with the communists who are causing all the trouble in the country. If we can all be Inkatha in this township there will be no fighting, no bloodshed."

My heart thudded, I felt light-headed.

My father spoke quietly. "You are asking for too much, my boy. Vusi here is still a student, as you know. He can't involve himself in these dangerous political enterprises."

"We are not asking him to leave the technikon. We value education, as you know from Dr Buthelezi's speeches. We are merely saying that in his spare time he can help recruit people for Inkatha. Inkatha is a responsible movement with a solid respectable history. Baba Khumalo, your wife is a Buthelezi, so is our leader, the Prince of Phindangene." Nkehli had done his homework to know my mother's maiden name. "By joining Inkatha you will not be lost. You will be in the company of a movement that will protect your pride as a Zulu person. Your son reads political science at school. He knows the history of Inkatha."

My father turned to me in shock. "You read politics at school? I thought we were paying you to read how to be a newspaper man."

"No, Baba Khumalo," Nkehli intervened. "The boy is not making a fool of you. The rules of the school maintain that if you want to be a good newspaperman you must study politics. Politics makes the world go around. Politics is just one of many subjects that your son is doing as part of his training to be a newspaperman."

My father thought about this, taking his time before responding. "Look, my boys, this is not an easy matter. Why don't you give us time to think it over?"

Smiling, Nkehli and his men got up and shook hands with my father. It was as if I wasn't there.

No sooner had they left than my father gave me money and told me to go back to my aunt in town. I knew my life was in danger. But the thought of going back to auntie's dingy room, sitting there like Emile Zola's condemned horse, depressed me.

As a word of advice my father said, "Don't show your face in the township until further notice."

# *Cosmopolitan* here I come!

AFTER MISSING SO MANY CLASSES it became difficult to go back to the technikon. When I did, my white classmates kept their distance, while the political science lecturer tried to tell me the fighting that had escalated in the townships was intertribal – Zulus against Xhosas.

"The cleavages are informed by tribal differences. These things are of an ethnic manifestation," he would lisp.

What irritated me most was that this sour-faced man criticised my use of English while ignoring the mangled language of other second-language students, particularly the Afrikaans students. None of my other teachers ever found fault with my English submissions, but this man would express his surprise when I passed the semesters and the end of year exam.

During the Christmas holiday I went back home but kept a low profile, although I did visit Mafika Gwala. He was reading by candlelight, all the curtains drawn. Outside was broad daylight.

"A person cannot live like this, Bhuti Pascal," I lamented. "I can't keep running away like this from these people."

"What do you propose to do?"

"I don't know. You know better. You are connected with the underground. I want to get out of the country. Get me out of the country."

"What?" He glared at me. "Are you out of your mind? How's that going to help you? The fighters are coming back from exile to escalate the fight and you want to run away. You want to be caught in the crossfire as you run away? Haven't you been listening. The boers are intercepting people either as they come in or go out. Killing them. Killing them left, right and centre!"

"There's no use sitting here, waiting for them. I mean making petrol bombs and throwing these at them is not enough. I can't use a gun properly. I am no match against these people!"

"Vusi, *phuma*! Out, out!" He opened the door.

I left. I knew the emotional turmoil I was causing him. What if he got me hooked up with people who could smuggle me out and I got killed along the way? What if I was working for the system, trying to get out of him the names and addresses of people in the underground? Who could you trust? The townships were awash with police spies.

I went home dejected. Days before the technikon re-opened, I moved in with my aunt again. I was determined to do even better in the second year, and began publishing articles in a number of regional newspapers – *The Daily News, Ilanga* and *Imvo Zabantsundu*. As my friend Fred Kockott had quit classes and was now running the technikon newspaper full time, I published there too, but concentrated on the paying markets.

My proudest moment, however, came when an opinion piece that I had written was pronounced the best in our group and forwarded to *Cosmopolitan* for possible publication.

At about the same time we were taken to visit Alan Paton. The celebrated author led a tranquil existence in the picturesque Valley of a Thousand Hills and I was overjoyed at the prospect of meeting him.

Makhokhoba, as Paton was called by close friends and former inmates of the Diepkloof Reformatory where had served as principal, welcomed us warmly into his house. His wife Margaret served tea and cakes, and we made ourselves comfortable. Some of the group circulated around his study, marvelling at his book collection.

We asked some stupid questions which must have irritated him, but Paton had the patience and forbearing of a saint.

"What do you think of Nadine Gordimer's books? Don't you think they lack human warmth?"

"How does one write a poem? Does one first think of a theme, or does one first decide the form it will take, whether it's going to be a sonnet or a limerick?"

"Why haven't you been harassed by the security police while so many other writers in the country have been victimised and jailed?"

Our lecturer intervened with a question. "In *Cry, The Beloved Country*

161

you warned that the government had refused to listen to the oppressed people's entreaties for equal rights and justice. You further warned that there would come a time when the government would remember that missed opportunity, when it would be on its knees trying to appeal for order, sanity. Have we reached that point of no return yet, when the victim has decided he has nothing to lose, when the victim is unleashing terror upon the former oppressor?"

To which Paton said, "I am afraid we've reached that point of no return. But naturally, in expressing their anger, the black people of this country are lashing out at everything and anything, hurting themselves in the process."

"What can be done now? Or is it just too late?"

"I know my friend Dr Buthelezi is trying his best to talk to the other side, the government, and also the ANC. But the government is thwarting all those efforts. It's a confused and confusing picture. In the process Dr Buthelezi is being painted as a traitor by a section of his own people. God knows he is trying his best to make things work. But his hands are tied. The government is still very much in power, and is putting a spanner in the works. Look, how many peace meetings have Dr Buthelezi's people held with the UDF? Countless. But all these efforts are thwarted by some force, some invisible hand that doesn't want peace."

On the drive back to Durban, I felt that Paton had become an apologist for Inkatha brutality.

A few weeks later I received a letter from *Cosmopolitan* accepting my article for publication. I read the letter over and over, clutching the cheque they'd sent. A cheque for R150. I couldn't believe it. Imagine a twenty-year-old black man having his work and his *picture* published in a lily-white woman's magazine! More than that, I could have rented a decent room in a commune on the Berea for two months with that money. But sense prevailed. I continued staying with my aunt.

I did buy a rickety typewriter with a few missing keys. In the afternoons, before auntie came back from work, I would sit on an old beer crate, a chair as my desk, and type my essays. On weekends, when my aunt was off visiting her boyfriend, I would clack away almost non-stop from morning to past midnight, writing newspaper articles and short stories. Money generated through freelance writing made a lot of difference. I could proudly contribute towards our groceries.

If there was a loss during the first half of the year, it was of my long-standing girlfriend to a man who immediately married her. Smarting from this I went home during the mid-term holidays to lick my wounds. My visit to the township turned out to be most traumatic.

# The making of a killer

THILO MKHIZE was the only guy I have ever known who fucked chickens. We were still boys back then, younger than ten years old.

I couldn't understand why he would want do to this, but then Thilo was no ordinary boy.

In primary school we were told that a frog could continue living days after you'd removed its heart. After school Thilo challenged us to go hunting for frogs. We caught about four and Thilo cut them open and removed the hearts. The frogs were placed in a box and next day were still alive. Thilo next wanted to experiment on a cat. When we said that was going too far, he cursed us for cowards.

Thilo had a drive for destruction. As there were stories doing the rounds that our school principal had staged a burglary of his own office to finance his new sleek Mercedes-Benz, Thilo wanted to stone the principal's car and burn down the school. Again we told him this was a crazy idea and threatened to blow the whistle on him should he go ahead.

A month later a lone figure was seen hurling a brick through the windscreen of the principal's car as he drove out of the school one night. The principal didn't make a big issue of it, but reminded us that he came from Swaziland, a land notorious for its powerful medicine men. He would cast a spell on the culprit. However, the culprit was never caught.

Thilo didn't do well at school. His father spent long stretches away from the family, his mother was dead, and his eldest brother spent more time in jail than out. Thilo quit school at an early age.

He found odd jobs working initially as a packer at a local shop where he stole items of grocery which a number of us then sold, cutting him into the takings. Because he was funny and talkative, customers loved him. The shop owner, a burly man, realised that he had a magnetic pull on customers so he soon graduated to the position of cashier.

Thilo became fatter. He kitted himself out in expensive fashionable clothes.

Somehow the shop owner cottoned on to what was happening to his money, and beat Thilo black and blue. When I next saw him Thilo's eyes were swollen closed, his shaven head looked as tender as a brinjal, his speech slurred, he walked like an old man.

Many thought Thilo had always been short of a few marbles, but after the beating he was never to be the same again.

He now had violent mood swings. He would crack a good joke, then when people laughed would suddenly start punching and kicking them, saying, "You think I can't see that you're laughing at me? You think the shop owner made me mad with his punches and boots?"

Over the years Thilo Mkhize turned into a violent thief. With the political violence of the 1980s, he had an outlet for his need to spill blood. He became one of the most feared fighters. And as our section of the township was dominated by the UDF, that meant he became a Comrade, frequently to be found in the streets beating up children on their way to school.

I saw Thilo at his worst during the 1986 mid-term break. It was a Saturday. I was in our lounge reading when a commotion started in the street. I got up to investigate and saw a man pursued by a group of boys. At the head of the chase was Thilo, yelling, "Catch the criminal! Catch the criminal!"

I joined the excited crowd. The fleeing man tripped and fell. He rose quickly, hands in the air, pleading, but his voice was drowned by the cries of the crowd.

The first brick caught the man smack in the face. He went down like a sack of maize. All the attackers were friends of mine. In the swirl of voices I learned that the man had killed a close friend and neighbour of ours, and this angered me. I was about to join the attack when a hand grabbed me roughly on my right shoulder. It was my father.

"Where do you think you are going?"

I paused.

"You think you are tough now? You are going to join the scavengers, spill blood. Do you know who it is that is being attacked, and for what reason?" Silence. Shame. From an early age, my father had not only taught me how to fight, but also when not to fight. Don't hit a person from behind – *ukuzuma*. Don't *hlanganyela* – a group of people ganging up against one person. A fight should always be one on one. Although he never encouraged us to run away from a fight – in fact he would cane me for not standing up for myself – he, paradoxically, told me it was healthy to be scared.

So we stood there in the street, father and son, watching as the assault continued. Rocks rained on the prone form; the man had lost consciousness.

"Hold on now! Stop!" Thilo shouted the command, obviously the leader. By now I had learnt that this man had accused our neighbour of being a police spy and struck him with a stick. Our neighbour had collapsed and died instantly.

Thilo sent a boy to fetch a bucket of water and this was dashed in the unconscious man's face. He came to his senses, his body trembling with fear. Someone came running with a car tyre. There were whistles of excitement, and shouts of: *"Shisa inja! Shisa inja!"* Burn the dog! Burn the dog! The tyre was placed around the man's neck and filled with petrol. Throughout a woman pleaded with the boys to spare the man until they screamed angrily at her, "What size of necklace do you take?" Then she turned on her heels and fled. More people came forward to beg for the man's life. They, too, were threatened. The boys were wild. It was difficult to believe that these were the boys I had played soccer with. The same boys I had roasted rats with. The same boys I had swam with at Umncadodo River.

Somebody threw a match onto the bloodied man. My father took my hand and we walked home. From our yard we watched as the human torch writhed on the road.

Later, the police came to pick up the remains. No one was arrested. No questions were asked. The man became another statistic of the political violence.

# Whites only

MY PARENTS WERE OVERJOYED when I completed my studies. But now I had to serve a year's internship with a media organisation before the technikon would award the diploma.

Almost all my white classmates found openings at *The Daily News* or *The Natal Mercury* but my letters of application to these newspapers came back regretfully pointing out that I had no experience.

Except that one of the senior editors at *The Daily News* called me for an interview. I went, my hopes high. The size of the newsroom was impressive: an array of desks with huge computers on them. I had never used a computer before. At the technikon they had trained us on typewriters. The prospect of using one of those gleaming monsters was enough to make me salivate.

As I walked towards the editor's office as directed by the white receptionist, I realised that everyone in the newsroom was white. It was a relief to see two black men dressed in uniform and probably messengers or drivers, but men I could greet in my own language.

The editor welcomed me with a warm smile, invited me to sit down. I offered him a file with my newspaper clippings. He ignored the file and continued talking about the news of the day. He asked a few questions to test my knowledge of current affairs: what did I think of the black on black violence? What did I think of sanctions that had been imposed by some overseas countries on South Africa? Were overseas companies right to disinvest from our country in a bid to force the apartheid government to its knees? Then he wanted to know about my background and my ambitions. Within five minutes the interview was over. He shook my hand. "Maybe you want to try one of the black papers. Try *Ilanga*," he said.

The absence of black faces in the newsroom drove home an important point. *The Daily News* had no hope of reporting stories that truly

167

reflected what was happening in the country. Their stories couldn't and wouldn't be able to capture the black point of view or understand the complexities of what was happening in the townships. The paper's white reporters were disadvantaged by their inability to speak our languages. But more importantly, a white person going to the township was always suspect. He could be a policeman or some agent of the hated government. His presence elicited fear or hate. Black people either ran away at the sight of him, or attacked him with angry words – *"hheyi, msunu kanyoko! Ufunani la?"*, or threw stones and other missiles.

On my way out of the newsroom I bumped into a black fellow with a light complexion and a bushy beard, dressed in a pair of smart pants, a white shirt and a tie. I greeted him tentatively in township lingo, *"Heita."*

*"Hoezit?"* he responded warmly. I introduced myself and explained that I had been for an interview. He said he'd trained at my alma mater not many years previously and was on the paper's editorial staff. Out of some seventy reporters, sub-editors and senior editors he was the only black person. The brother had a look about him that showed he was lonely. When I told him what his boss had said as a parting shot, he laughed long and loud.

"Welcome to our reality!" he said. We shook hands and parted.

I had been told to look beyond the façade of liberalism that adorned the English-language publishing establishment. I had been told that there were huge salary gaps between blacks and whites working for these newspapers.

Newspapers like *Ilanga* and *Sowetan*, though owned by the Argus group which also owned *The Daily News*, were treated as poor cousins of the "white" newspapers. The "black" newspapers were the last to be computerised. Their staffers drove around in jalopies, while white journalists had good well-serviced cars at their disposal. The offices of black newspapers were located in dingy surroundings, while white newspapers were housed in roomy air-conditioned offices in the swanky part of town. For all the liberal noises, the white English-language publishing houses were racist.

Because my journalism training had been conducted in English, I wanted to work for an English-language newspaper. I was more comfortable writing in English. Besides, there were only two Zulu-language newspapers in the country whereas English-language papers were published in every major city.

When *The Daily News* editor made it clear to me that I was not welcome in the white journalistic world, initially I was hurt. At technikon I had proved that I was better than most of the white students, but the publishing industry didn't think so.

It left no alternative but to apply to a black newspaper. I sent a letter to Obed Kunene, the editor of *Ilanga*. He responded promptly, inviting me to his office for an interview.

Kunene was from the old school. Although the newspaper published in Zulu, he conducted his business with his staff in formal English. That I had contributed on a freelance basis to his paper impressed him immensely. He was satisfied that I could write and I understood the issues that touched the lives of his constituency. He offered me a job on the spot. The downside, however, was that the only job available was as a sports reporter. My father's disastrous obsession with soccer had created in me a passionate aversion to sports. Nevertheless, I took the job.

Within a few months I was thoroughly enjoying myself. I was learning, the senior journalists were eager to help, and the newsroom had a spirit of warm camaraderie. Our desks were rickety, probably hand-me-downs from the white paper, ditto the typewriters, but what mattered was the ethos. Our political affiliations differed but we could argue our positions openly, which we would not have been able to do on a white newspaper. I heard stories of how editors on white newspapers in Johannesburg spiked the copy their black reporters had risked their lives to get. Many felt the editors kept tabs on black reporters and alerted the authorities to the more revolutionary types. I began to thank *The Daily News* editor for barring me from the white press.

# Debauchery at Snake Park

I WORKED HARD, not only writing sports stories, but producing copy for the main section of the paper: politics, general news, entertainment, the odd book review. I wanted to impress the editors, more importantly, I wanted out of the sports ghetto. My diligence paid off. Before the year was over, I was transferred to the newsroom.

If these were heady days on the paper, they were no less so socially. I was living, illegally of course, in Berea in a commune I shared with a bunch of white youngsters. Some of them had been at technikon with me. Leslie was a journalism drop-out who lived with her boyfriend Mark. Mark was an affable little fellow with not much to say unless he was talking about snakes. On Saturdays he would hunt through the veld for snakes, usually returning with a few in a bag. These then joined his collection in a glass tank. Hence the reason our digs earned the sobriquet Snake Park. Apart from Mark and Leslie, a number of other people drifted in and out of the house and you almost never knew who was a permanent resident and who an interloper.

Initially I was the only darkie, but then Sipho Khumalo, my loud-mouthed distant brother, moved in and livened up the house with his weird political observations. I sometimes wondered if the security police wouldn't be alerted to the real and present danger posed to society by this angry black brother at Snake Park.

Apart from being a great place for political debates, we refined our skills in debauchery. There was a parade of women eager to be pleased, rivers of alcohol begging to be consumed, forests of dagga waiting to be smoked. I had always thought that white people regarded their bodies, in the biblical sense, as God's temples, that they ingested only what was healthy and holy. My stay at Snake Park opened my eyes to new realities.

As a youngster I had been shocked by black people who drank *isqatha* –

that concoction of potato peels, yeast, breadcrumbs, car battery acid and sometimes benzine. At Snake Park I discovered that white people could get equally creative in their quest for the highest possible state of intoxication. After consuming bottles of tequila, they would bake cakes seasoned with generous dollops of dagga. These we would have for supper most weekends. The first time I ate a dagga cake I went stark raving mad. We were listening to Bob Dylan, smoking weed and eating dagga cake. I suddenly heard loud noises as if a warplane had fallen on our roof. The walls collapsed before my eyes. I got up, screaming and punching the air. Leslie and another girl had to hold my hands and calm me down as I tried to run away from the crumbling walls.

We had occasional visits from the police who once or twice confiscated fistfuls of dagga. But they never arrested anyone. The Group Areas Act was still in force, but I could sense that the young white cops were tired of the stupidity of some of the laws they had to enforce.

If booze and dagga were plentiful at Snake Park, food was scarce. It wasn't as if we didn't have money to buy groceries, it was that we lacked the time and inspiration to cook. At first I took it upon myself to cook for everybody. But it became clear that no one appreciated my culinary expertise. No one ever said, "Thanks, Fred, that was a nice meal", or "Stay as far away from the kitchen as possible, Fred, because you can't bloody cook!" No. They just kept quiet and gobbled my food.

After eating, they failed to wash the dishes. Because I couldn't live among piles of unwashed dishes, I did the washing up as well. Until one day I decided, fuck it, these whiteys think I'm their houseboy. I stopped cooking.

Leslie complained that she missed my cooking. I responded by giving her cooking lessons.

My stay with the white denizens of Snake Park, waking up in the same house with them, eating with them, drinking with them, fighting with them, fucking with them, opened a window into the lives of "the other half". It also showed me how little whites knew about us. These people were educated, well travelled and open-minded, but black

171

people continued to puzzle them. The system had succeeded in making them fear and mistrust black people. In that sense it had denied them their humanity. I also realised that at a basic level blacks knew more about whites. We spoke their language, while not many of them could even greet me in Zulu. We knew the houses and the neighbourhoods in which they lived, yet how many whites had visited a township let alone been inside a black home. Our mothers cooked for them, nursed their children, yet they never asked if black mothers had enough time with their own children.

But Snake Park also showed me that, like me, the white kids were frustrated with the conditions that had been imposed upon them by the apartheid government. Some of them had joined the End Conscription Campaign and faced jail sentences if they refused to report for their obligatory army service. I had always thought that blacks were the only victims of apartheid. But at that house I saw many young white men collapsing under the yoke of apartheid. Angry with the laws of the country, but powerless to wage a sustainable war against the apartheid regime, many of those youngsters turned their anger on themselves. They drank too much, smoked too much, and never seemed to think about the future. Many of them had dropped out of technikon or university. They didn't seem to be serious about finding work either. They lived the lives of vagabonds. A couple became serious drug addicts, an affliction that endures to this day. Life at that house made me better appreciate the rage, frustration and impotence that must have consumed Allen Ginsberg, the Beat poet, when he wrote his famous poem "Howl": *I saw the best minds of my generation destroyed . . .*

I realised that while Thilo had grown up to be an angry social misfit, the white kids I was living with had internalised their anger. They waged a psychological war on themselves. They wrecked their brains and bodies with booze and drugs. They starved themselves of food and spiritual sustenance. In a way, we were all victims of the system.

I hadn't been on *Ilanga* long when it was sold to Inkatha. I couldn't work for a paper owned by a political party, especially a political party in the service of the apartheid regime.

Dr Oscar Dhlomo, then general secretary of Inkatha and also chairman of Mandla/Matla, the publishing wing of the party, assured us that there would be no editorial interference. That was cold comfort. Most of the reporters were worried about the association with the party. We also feared for our lives. We resigned en masse. It was a traumatic experience, especially for people who had been at the paper for decades. Some of them did not have the qualifications to move to other newspapers, besides, the only other Zulu paper was *UmAfrika*, a small church-owned weekly. For many veterans who couldn't write in English, the purchase of *Ilanga* by Inkatha marked the end of the road.

# Writing or fighting?

"Words are our only weapon
in our long quarrel with God."
PETER COLLIER, *Los Angeles Times Book Review*

BEING A BLACK JOURNALIST in the late 1980s was difficult. You were harassed by the police and intelligence networks, while the black community often thought you were in cahoots with the system. Then there were the political organisations. If you were seen as being too close to one party, you became persona non grata with the others.

Every time I interviewed a senior government official or an Inkatha leader my neighbours in the township wondered if I was trading information, after all, I came from a UDF neighbourhood. Whereas once the Inkatha people knew my background they wondered if I was spying on them.

I recall that journalists on the *Sowetan* were perceived to be Azapo, and therefore anti-UDF, so they couldn't cover UDF events. In fact, in some townships the paper could not be sold as local activists would attack vendors who sold this "reactionary" newspaper.

After resigning from *Ilanga*, I joined *UmAfrika*, owned by the MMI order of Catholic priests and funded by overseas anti-apartheid organisations. The paper had first appeared at the beginning of the twentieth century, its express aim being to spread Christianity and encourage education among black people.

When I joined *UmAfrika* the paper was a rag of no consequence. While the country went up in flames, the editor of *UmAfrika* led with stories on baptisms, confirmations and obituaries of prominent priests and church luminaries. Stories culled from the news services and translated into Zulu were the paper's most ambitious attempt at being a mirror of what was happening in the country.

The paper printed about four thousand copies a week which were given away to parishioners around the province. Ordinary newspaper readers refused to buy it or accept it as a free sheet.

However, the owners were concerned about the criticism and realised the paper had to be repositioned. They hired an editorial consultant from the defunct *Rand Daily Mail* who worked in close conjunction with the University of Natal's Centre for Contemporary Cultural Studies. Part of the repositioning strategy was to recruit young black journalists. I was one of these. As was my friend and former classmate, Chris Hlongwa. The editor, Anthony Ndlovu, an avuncular old man who had been there for twenty years, was replaced by Cyril Madlala, *Ilanga*'s labour and political reporter.

When Madlala took over, Ndlovu continued editing the racing page while other long-standing editorial staff quickly adapted to the new ethic.

Although the owners weren't entirely happy with the new direction, *UmAfrika* grew into a feisty paper selling sixty thousand copies a week. The publishing industry took note. The politicians took note. The political movements battled to win our favour.

It was a young newsroom. I was not yet twenty-one when I joined, most of the others were in their mid- to late twenties. We were energetic, committed. We had to be prepared to turn our hands to reporting, editing, designing, taking photographs. The experience was stimulating: each one of us could have produced the newspaper by himself.

Madlala's genius as editor soon manifested itself. He offered the various political organisations space to argue their positions. *UmAfrika* became a nation talking to itself. Senior lecturers from universities in the province contributed their analyses of the political situation while students chose *UmAfrika* as the subject of their theses. But our balanced reporting, our erudition, our fairness did not guarantee us immunity from those who thought we were pushing the line of the "enemy camp". Our journalists were abused, threatened, insulted.

Publishing in Zulu was unfortunate because it restricted the market, but that did not stop independent newspapers such as the *Weekly Mail*, *South* and *New Nation* from asking us to translate many of our features so that they could publish them. They also joined with *UmAfrika* editorial staff on some long-term investigative projects.

The success of *UmAfrika* as an alternative voice to the mainstream Natal press encouraged Scandinavian interests to launch an English newspaper in the province. Called *The New African,* it was jointly edited by Ricky Naidoo, my former classmate, and Sipho Khumalo, my former Snake Park housemate, with Clive Emdon as writer and editorial advisor. The link with *UmAfrika* was paramount and many of us were on the founding editorial committee. Unfortunately *The New African* was not as successful as *UmAfrika*. Advertisers took one look and ran, claiming that the paper was too political. Circulation was paltry. Nevertheless, while the paper lasted it offered some of us an opportunity to publish in English, and I wrote profiles of jazz stars, book reviews and a no-holds-barred column called Firing Line. My friends and colleagues who were passionate about music had deepened my understanding of jazz, an appreciation that had been started by Mafika Gwala. Consequently I was able to write with authority and passion about both local and international jazz trends and personalities.

Gwala had led me to John Coltrane and, through his music, Coltrane taught me about the freedom of the spirit, about respect for oneself, and about a love for one's fellow human beings. The man's legacy changed my life, so that when times were bleak I turned to his music or read his biographies which never failed to uplift my spirits. Coltrane helped me understand my tragic existence. He triggered questions, aroused doubts and suspicions.

Because of him, I began to flirt with the Hare Krishna movement in search of spiritual fulfilment. From a young age, I was always on the lookout for a source of spiritual sustenance. I felt the urge to connect with a super power, the all-knowing entity that decided man's destiny. No matter how much I prayed at church, I never reached the desired high, did not entirely connect with that elusive super being. I turned to the Hare Krishna movement and attended services at their temple in Chatsworth. For a while, I was consumed by the movement. I stopped eating meat, stopped drinking in keeping with Sanskrit scriptures. It was a fulfilling period, spiritually and psychologically. I felt cleaner. But I also knew that my friends could not understand my obsessions. Still, I had more time to myself; I read more. That in turn opened floodgates of creativity.

My profile as a prolific and versatile writer did not go unnoticed by editors in Johannesburg. I received invitations to contribute to influential national magazines such as *Tribute, Pace* and *Drum.*

Because the pool of celebrities was so shallow in the black community, I almost immediately became a celebrity. I was invited to give motivational speeches to schoolchildren and members of youth societies around the province. People thought I was the sharpest tongued columnist around and a knowledgeable reviewer.

These compliments did not satisfy my hunger for achievement. I knew that I was still learning the craft. I considered myself a hack; I wanted to be a writer. I produced short stories and poetry which were published in local publications such as *Echo*, the "black" supplement of the white mainstream newspaper *The Natal Witness.*

But the blood flowing wherever I turned continued to be a psychological torment, a major distraction. I couldn't sit down and write, pretending everything was hunky dory in my community, in my country. Abruptly I curtailed my flirtation with the Hare Krishna movement. The reality around me was too much. I felt I couldn't have my head in the clouds, float about on a spiritual high while people were dying around me.

There were moral questions too. Should the writer sit back, observe and record the fighting unfolding before him? Or should he abandon writing – some people thought it was a bourgeois preoccupation anyway – and get on with the fight? Or could the writer do both?

More often than not, I was ready to fight. Early in 1989, for example, word went around that our neighbourhood would be attacked by Inkatha. A group of young men and boys decided to mount a vigil through the night. We made petrol bombs, then smashed the street lights until the neighbourhood was plunged into darkness. Everyone had been warned to keep off the streets.

The group I was with waited in a clump of trees near the reservoir across the road from my house. At about ten o'clock the heavy dud-dud-dud-dud of a helicopter filled the sky. We reached for our petrol bombs, watching the helicopter's searchlight tracking over the yards and streets. Someone must have told the police we had stockpiled petrol bombs. The helicopter came over low. We lay flat on our stomachs.

"Let's run for it!" somebody whispered. "They are going to land the bloody 'copter on top of us!"

"Don't move! You want them to start shooting us? Keep quiet!"

"Let's get up with our hands in the air!" The guy was sobbing, ready to run. We pinned him to the ground, clamped a hand across his mouth.

"The minute they jump off that bloody thing, we throw our petrol bombs, burn them!" someone shouted.

I could see a man leaning from the helicopter, getting ready to jump.

But then the helicopter climbed away and disappeared into the night. We laughed with relief.

It was agreed that each person should take his petrol bombs and find a hiding place for them. As we walked away from the reservoir we began wondering aloud who had told the police about our strategy.

At about one a.m. we decided that Inkatha wasn't coming. Nevertheless, we waited for daybreak, drinking beer to pass the time.

Later, I realised that if I had been caught by the police, and they had discovered I was a newspaperman, my career might have ended. But the question wouldn't go away: to write or to fight?

Some writers felt you could do both. Ben Dikobe Martins, for example, had been arrested for "acts of terror". Ronnie Kasrils, a prolific poet, was a senior member of Umkhonto we Sizwe. On the other hand Mafika Gwala had argued against my joining the fighters. And I had never seen reason to oppose his point of view. Maybe in my heart of hearts I knew that I wanted to write, first and foremost. Fighting physically would be incidental.

I was not the first South African writer, of course, to be faced with the dilemma of whether to fight or to write. Many before me had raised the issue, and I thought particularly of the lines in Arthur Nortje's "Native's Letter":

For some of us must storm the castles
some define the happening.

I kept reminding myself that I had chosen to "define the happening"
even though the urge to go "storming the castles" was constant. Because of the violence and the restlessness in the country, I found that
I couldn't concentrate on my craft as much as I wanted to. The restlessness informed what I wrote. In late 1989 I published a poem called
"Ghastly Choreographers" in *Staffrider:*

The chilly pitch-black night
enters the dark bottomless hole
of my head.

Filtering through the seams
Of my window are shrill,
Ghastly shrieks
– I can't help but
take a cautious peep.

There, out there
Blazing white forms
stain this charcoal night.

The ghastly choreographers
Wriggle and wallow
in this pitch-black night
evoking in me a trepidation
that conquers my consciousness
– I slip into sleep.

When I read the poem today, I relive the fear and psychological un-
ease, the breathless intensity of the time, and the days that were to
follow.

The poem, like many other pieces of creative writing that I have produced over the years, reminds me of my mentor Mafika Gwala.

My relationship with Gwala became intermittent as the violence swirled across the province. Whereas I'd tried to see him as often as possible, at the height of the violence I couldn't find him. He was never at his house. Some said he had fled to his ancestral village in Intshanga, others said he was staying with friends in the nearby township of KwaNdengezi. Eventually, when the violence petered out he suddenly reappeared and we met at his house. Mafika had never been a snazzy dresser; he did not care about appearances. But over the years he had become more slovenly. He hardly shaved, or combed his hair. His glasses were smudged. His lips were cracked, the result of his excessive liquor consumption.

"Ah, Vusi, my boy. I see you are doing well with the newspapers," he said. "Keep up the good work."

Yet our meetings were awkward, he was nervous, uneasy in my presence, possibly embarrassed with the way he looked. Whenever I talked about writing or politics, he would change the subject. He wanted us to dwell in shallow generalisations about how our township had deteriorated. He couldn't have been writing anything of consequence, which was sad, because his last volume of poems, *No More Lullabies,* published in 1982, had been well received. He had continued to write the occasional essay or short story ( some of which were published in *Staffrider*, and other literary journals), but his enthusiasm for literary work had ebbed. The violence had a lot to do with his statelessness – physically and psychologically. But booze had also taken its toll. His house was chaotic, and at the height of the violence it had been used as a hideout by mean-looking youths who had no idea what a literary giant the man was. They had stayed on, and were smoking and drinking noisily in the yard, paying very little respect to their host, on one occasion when I visited. This all pained me. I wished we could recreate those wonderfully heated literary debates we'd had in his house. I wished the Mpumalanga Arts Ensemble could be resuscitated. But it was too late. The members were now scattered all over the world.

# Falling in love again

AFTER LOSING MY CHILDHOOD SWEETHEART, I had a stream of flings and one night stands. My disappointment at my childhood sweetheart would henceforth influence the way I related to women. I was distrusting and sceptical. Maybe I had been naïve to think my affair with my childhood sweetheart would blossom into a fully-fledged romance that would lead to marriage. Perhaps as a way of "fighting back" at women, a procession of them went through my bed. Sometimes I would wake in the morning, my head heavy with a hangover, surprised to find some woman I didn't know sleeping beside me.

But my life changed when I met Mantombi Ndaba. She was a charming, outgoing woman. After the debauchery of Snake Park, life with the conservative Mantombi was quiet. I cut down on the booze, and almost did away with all the other stimulants.

Actually, after Snake Park was condemned by the council as structurally unsound (and subsequently demolished) I had moved into a commune with my old friend Fred Kockott. It was a clean, civilised place. The other residents cooked, dinner time was an occasion for getting together and talking, and afterwards we took turns at washing up.

Friends would come round for a party or a braai and we would get down to a lot of boozing and politicking. One night, late into the drinking session, one of the white guests told us, almost tearfully, that in the next few days he was scheduled for an army camp. He said he would have to serve in a township where there was "unrest". The atmosphere in the room turned sullen. Perhaps each of us was wondering how many black kids this white boy was going to kill, probably out of fear. And would he come out alive. Would he continue to converse and drink freely with us – especially the black component of the party – after his experiences in the army?

Such thoughts clustered around our lives, yet we still lived and loved.

I was happiest in Mantombi's presence. She had stayed for many years in my township, she understood my background. She helped keep me away from the fighting. She appreciated my interests – jazz, books, art, cinema. We visited art exhibitions, second-hand bookshops, and the library at the American Cultural Center. Some of the books in this collection were banned and not available at our public library, among them *Invisible Man* by Ralph Ellison and Mark Mathabane's hard-hitting autobiography *Kaffir Boy*. Here, too, we watched documentaries on the political situation in the country, many produced by American TV networks such as ABC. Because they exposed police brutality in the townships they were deemed subversive by government. In the twisted logic of the deputy minister of information "[t]here [was] no press censorship, but there [was] a limit to what [could] be published." Given this situation the American Cultural Center gave us news of what was happening in our own backyard.

We were also actively encouraged by those at the Center to apply for the various scholarships on offer at American universities. I wrote off to a number and the subsequent exchange of letters with Columbia University excited my interest. The university had an excellent master's programme in journalism, but Mantombi was disapproving from the onset.

"If you go to the US, who is going to take care of your brothers and sisters at home? You know as I know that your parents can't cope by themselves. There isn't enough money."

She was right. I was sending money home, but I also thought she was being myopic. She didn't see the bigger picture. Through achieving my dream of an overseas education, I would be in an even better position to send more generous contributions to my parents when I came back home.

One day she put it very bluntly: if you leave for the US, I'll find another man.

We had a major fight.

Not long afterwards she discovered that she was pregnant. Although it was unplanned we never considered terminating the pregnancy. In fact the pregnancy brought back a semblance of happiness which we hadn't experienced since the fight over my ambitions to study overseas.

We moved from one commune into another, and it was here that my daughter Noluthando was born. But despite the joy over the baby I felt sad that she had come into being at this unhappy juncture in my life, and in the life of my country. There was no place she could call home as we were always on the move. The laws of the white man kept us on our toes. We were like hunted rabbits.

Noluthando was a few months old when Mantombi and I started fighting again. We were inexorably drifting apart, and it pained me because I still loved her although she drove me crazy with her refusal to think logically about the bigger picture.

I shouldn't have allowed Mantombi to prevent me from taking up a bursary to a United States university. Emboldened by my acquiescence, she said "no" to everything and anything I suggested. Because she hadn't finished high school, I urged her to matriculate, but she refused, arguing that she was too old to go back to school. I told her it wasn't one of my ambitions to live with a person who had no vision for the future, no dreams, no focus. She just shrugged off my frustrated cry for reason. And the fighting went on.

I was also unhappy about Noluthando's "illegitimate" status. I had been raised in a solid family and I didn't want to deviate from that noble tradition. I didn't want to contribute to the shameful trend of single parenthood. But I could only do so much. Ultimately, Mantombi moved out, and went to stay with her parents.

I then met and started living with a bright woman who understood me all too well. Jacqui was a trained psychologist, she could delve into the darkest corners of my mind and fish from there my darkest fears, my secrets. She was almost my shrink. I used to unburden myself to her. I used to share my ambitions with her. With her, I used to dream.

"You can't keep trying to be a hero," she would say, "for a person your age you've done enough to open people's eyes, showing them the folly of their ways. (I was twenty-two going on twenty-three then.) Take a break, go and learn some more. Maybe by the time you come back things

183

will have changed. Things can't go on like this forever. But you can't change things single-handedly. Your township as it is now is not good for your state of mind. You can't keep trying to save people who don't want to be saved. Walk away, sweetheart, walk away. You need a break. Walk away."

But before I could do that Inkatha launched a devastating attack.

# Give us guns, not newspaper reports

EARLY IN APRIL 1990, almost two months after the release of Nelson Mandela, the violence was everywhere. Almost every day new outrages were reported. Each one more brutal than the last. In March, Pietermaritzburg had been the focal point of the violence. Newspaper headlines screamed: "Natal on the boil", "Thousands in impi attack"; "'War' in Maritzburg". There were stories of murder, displacement, dispossession. It was estimated that some twelve thousand men armed with guns and sub-machine guns were involved in the violence, repeatedly attacking the townships of Ashdown, Vulisaka, KwaMnyandu, Caluza, KwaShange, Gezubuso. This upsurge of violence became known as the Seven Days War.

Now the violence moved south towards our township.

Rumours had it that Inkatha threatened Mpumalanga with the war to end all wars on 4 April. Two things made the threat sound real: recently Inkatha had lost its leader Zakhele Nkehli, and many people fleeing war-torn Pietermaritzburg and the surrounding areas had sought refuge in our township. It was therefore to be expected that the violence would follow them.

Nkehli had died after a high speed car chase through Mpumalanga. Shortly before Christmas 1989 he had been driving home with his sister and wife when the chase began, his assailants firing repeatedly at his car until he lost control and crashed. Although he was only to die of his injuries some days later, his sister was killed instantly and his wife suffered injuries. Inkatha had reason to spill blood to avenge his murder.

To give some insight into the nature of the violence, and the violence of Nkehli, it is necessary to tell a chilling story I had covered for the newspaper a year previously. Two women, Stella Msomi and Sihle Ncala, had been kidnapped, raped and left for dead with their throats slit.

Ncala died but Msomi lived to tell the tale. Both these women were known to me, they were neighbours, as was the perpetrator. Msomi told the police that she and Ncala had been suspected of spying on Inkatha. As punishment they were kidnapped from their homes, taken to a house, bound with ropes, raped repeatedly, and then had their throats slit. She accused one Nyoni Hlongwane of the deed.

Those of us who knew Nyoni were shocked. We published the story without naming him, but he was subsequently arrested and appeared in court. He told a stunned judge that he had been trained as an Inkatha hit man in the battle against the UDF. He said he had been instructed by Nkehli to murder the two women. Specifically he had been instructed to make the women suffer, they had to beg for their lives. They had to scream loud and long. He fortified himself with muti to protect himself from being arrested on the understanding that the potency of the muti depended on the suffering of the women. The louder they screamed, the stronger would be the muti. In obedience to Nkehli's instructions, Nyoni chose to slit Sihle Ncala's throat while Stella Msomi watched. He told the court that he had done this slowly, and that both women had screamed as the blade ate into their throats.

He was found guilty and sentenced to life imprisonment. Years later, in an application for amnesty against possible prosecution in relation to other murders which had been uncovered and linked to him, Nyoni would shock the nation again. He admitted to murdering at least sixty people in the war between Inkatha and the UDF, including his own cousin who was a UDF gunman. On some occasions, Nyoni testified, he would kill two or three people at a scene. On many of these killing missions he was accompanied by one of the young men who had come with Nkehli in his attempt to pressurise me into joining Inkatha.

The Truth and Reconciliation Commission granted Nyoni amnesty for the sixty-odd murders, but denied amnesty for the murder of Ncala and attempted murder of Msomi.

When the day for the "war to end all wars" dawned, I was in the newsroom working on a story. I received a call from the daughter of that famous businessman of old and now a powerful UDF leader, Mcoyi, that the police were unusually busy and that there might be something going on. Because it was a Thursday, a slack day in our weekly schedule, I decided to drive out to Mpumalanga early in the afternoon.

"They are not fighting there today, are they?" asked Baba Kunene, the newspaper's driver, as we walked casually to the car.

"No," said I, "we're just doing our routine checks. We'll hit one or two beers there once we've ascertained with all the sources that there's nothing wrong."

When we arrived in the township everything seemed normal. At the Methodist church a group of people, including the Reverend Ngcibi, were holding a meeting. Apart from his priestly duties, Ngcibi was also involved in politics and was said to make frequent trips to the Eastern Cape to collect guns and fighters. I never questioned these allegations; some things it was safer not to know about.

The discussions in the church hall revolved around issues of safety. People were being assigned to keep lawyers updated about detentions and arrests. And then a sudden racket outside had us scrambling to our feet, those with guns cocked their weapons.

A teacher burst into the church, gun in hand. He was so excited he was gabbling: "Comeonpeoplethingsarebadnow!"

"What?"

He took a deep breath, and said, "They have arrived. Things are happening now. They have already started at Unit 3."

Everybody understood. Reverend Ngcibi issued instructions and asked for a man known as Sandlana to be fetched. Sandlana was one of the UDF/ANC's feared marksmen who, it was said, had killed more than thirty people since the fighting started. He and another sharpshooter (with only eleven hits under his belt) would sit on a ridge above the Inkatha-dominated area and wager on their marksmanship.

"I bet you R20 you can't hit that woman in red walking down that street."

"Let me show you what I can do," the other would say, looking into the scope of his .303. "I will not hit her, I will just hit the water bucket

187

that she's carrying on her head. Just to scare her." Then he would squeeze the trigger, indeed hitting the bucket on the woman's head. The frightened woman would spin around in confusion while up on the hill the two gunmen laughed uproariously, patting each other on the back.

While the meeting broke up, Baba Kunene and I drove off at high speed behind the armed teacher.

We stopped near my parents' house. Across the valley dark plumes of smoke spiralled up from the many burning houses. There were people running in the street, the continuous sound of gunfire, the explosions of petrol bombs.

The teacher took a large rifle from the boot of his car, handing me his handgun.

"Let's go!" he said.

"No!" I said, immediately giving him back the gun. He shrugged and ran directly towards the approaching attackers, firing his rifle into the throng. The attackers, who had met no serious challenge yet, scattered and retreated.

Camera in hand, I ran down a path that led to my street. Houses were on fire, a corpse lay at a neighbour's gate. I kept running. I thought I'd seen smoke and fire coming from my parents' house. I ran faster. I bumped into youths who recognised me and told me breathlessly, "Run the other way, the other way! Don't go home. *Otheleweni* [a pejorative word for Inkatha people] have descended upon the place. They are with the boers."

Across the valley I could see camouflage vehicles in the streets, and these were soon joined by two SA Defence Force vehicles. Also I had seen the police moving towards our neighbourhood, openly covering the armed Inkatha hordes hurling petrol bombs at houses they passed. The neighbourhood was enveloped in thick black smoke. There was more shooting. The marauders numbered around six hundred, shooting at anything that moved, breaking into houses, looting goods and setting the houses alight.

I started clicking away at the crowd and the burning houses. Then

I heard a voice calling out behind the haze of smoke, "There goes another dog."

There was a rat-a-tat of gunfire. I dived instinctively onto the tarred road, waited, then started up again and ran for my life. Another round of prolonged shooting forced me to take cover. Again I got up, bullets whizzing above my head, bullets slapping into the ground around me.

I ran, a police van close behind me, a man leaning out of the passenger window, his gun belching a torrent of bullets. It was dark now, the smoke of the burning houses obscuring the sun. Exhausted, gasping for breath, I threw myself into the bush and tall grass on the premises of Ingede Higher Primary School, my alma mater.

The van stopped a few metres from my hideout and two white cops scanned the area. After a few minutes they drove away and I noted the van's registration number: BFY434B.

(Later, my eyewitness report, including this number, was published in various newspapers such as the *Weekly Mail, Vrye Weekblad, South, New Nation* and my own *UmAfrika*. I wrote numerous letters to the police authorities trying to find out who was in the vehicle that day, but they never responded. In fact I was discouraged from pursuing the matter least I "disappear".)

But now, in the smoke and turmoil of the fighting, I emerged from my hideout only to be confronted by four panga-wielding youths. I stood rooted to the ground, watching death closing in on me.

But one of the youths recognised me and shouted excitedly, "Bhuti kaThabo, [Thabo's brother] run! They are now close by!"

His words were interrupted by another rattle of sub-machine gun fire. We all hit the ground.

Now I ran up the slope towards where Baba Kunene waited anxiously in the car, the engine running. We drove off.

On the way back to the office I was distraught. I had seen smoke coming from our house and the houses next to it. What had become of my sisters? By the time we got to the office, I was crying shamelessly. I thought I had seen it all, but I had never seen fighting as bad as this.

Later that evening I drove back to the township with a colleague. My home stood intact, a knot of people near the gate. The three houses opposite us had been burned severely, including that of the Malefanes.

Further down the street a neighbour lay dead in a pool of blood, his daughter screaming with grief, pounding the ground with her fists. I walked into our yard. My father and brother Bongani appeared and led me into the house which was sodden with water as a precaution against a petrol bomb. Also they had lifted all the carpets, doused them with water and dumped them in a corner. The children, they said, had fled to safety and were hiding with other women and children in the bush outside the township. Preparations were being made for them to be accommodated overnight in churches and schools.

My colleague and I then drove from street to street, where policemen questioned people and compiled statements in a manner so diligent that no one could credit that a few hours before they had openly collaborated with the attackers.

"The statements they pretend to be compiling are absolute nonsense because they are the ones who were killing our children and looting our property," a woman wailed.

"Yes," a young man shouted at a white policeman, pointing a finger threateningly, clearly having decided that he had nothing to lose now, "Yes, we know that you have been sent by Pretoria to revenge the death of Terblanche." (Captain Deon Terblanche, a senior officer with the Riot Squad, had been shot to death a week previously by his black junior, Roy Ngcobo, who lived in our part of the township. The black constable was himself shot dead by a white colleague a day later.)

Above the din, a local shebeen king moaned, "These bastards took all the beers in the fridge."

A gale of laughter met his misfortune.

We continued from street to street, interviewing people about their losses. This was, and will always be, the most difficult part of a reporter's job: asking people to relive their pain and loss. Asking people where they were going to sleep now that their house had been burnt down. Asking people if they had enough money to bury their dead. These questions always sound so mocking.

We counted more than a hundred burnt-out houses and five corpses. While people salvaged what they could from their destroyed homes, young men were already talking in quiet tones about the next move.

One of them told me derisively, "Groot man, we want guns, not newspaper reports. What use are newspapers? We will not use newspapers to hit back. We will beat them with guns."

Shortly after the 4 April massacre people felt the need for revenge. UDF fighters were summoned from surrounding townships. An *inyanga* made a pot of *intelezi*, a herb used by warriors in preparation for war. Each warrior was sprinkled with the mixture which would make them brave and fearsome in the face of the enemy and fortify them against enemy bullets. They then jumped over a huge fire, shouting, *"Ngadla mina!"* – I've hit him!

I wasn't there when the fighting started. But I learnt later that the attack had been well planned. Comrades went from house to house calling all the men to a meeting on an open piece of ground near Ingede Primary School.

Here, one of the gunmen mapped out the attack strategy. He planned to drive with a couple of other fighters at high speed through the Inkatha territory, shooting at random. The Inkatha fighters would retaliate by giving chase. The car would return to the UDF section and the pursuing Inkatha forces would be ambushed.

The attack went according to plan. By the time I arrived late in the afternoon, dense clouds of smoke boiled over the township and gunfire cracked everywhere. Organised and well-armed, our side had Inkatha on the retreat. I joined a bunch of neighbours. Every man had a weapon in his hand – a panga, a spear, a homemade gun, anything.

I saw a neighbour firing his home-made rifle like a madman until his weapon was too hot to handle. He passed it to the next warrior who wrapped a piece of cloth around it and continued firing.

"Our" side was divided into small groups that attacked from the flanks. Many hurled petrol bombs or threw stones. Some of the fighters were well trained and carried R1s and AK47s. Others had handguns. Among us were those whose hearts were revolted by what they were doing but who did it because they were there, having been born at the wrong place, at the wrong time.

For some reason, the police only arrived when it was all over. By then the no-man's land between our part of the township and the Inkatha section was littered with bodies, some still alive. People from both sides watched as the police solemnly picked up the bodies. Most of those watching were women. The men were ready to bolt should the police start their dirty tricks.

Among the policemen I recognised top black cops who were known to be neutral, unlike the white cops who always took sides. We relaxed. When we were asked to collect the wounded, both sides moved forward cautiously. Women screamed as they encountered their loved ones who were either dead or badly injured. Tensions were high and the police reluctant to arrest anyone for fear of sparking the violence all over again.

I found a friend who had been shot in the knee and was sitting among some bodies, bleeding badly. We rushed towards him.

"Over there," he said, pointing ahead of us. "Go and help Cebo over there. Leave me alone. I'll be able to cope. Cebo needs serious attention. I saw him fall."

We rushed towards where he had pointed. Indeed, it was Cebo Nxumalo, my former high school mate with whom I had argued about black consciousness.

Cebo lay on his back, his eyes looking at the sky. The bullets had shredded his rib cage. Blood bubbled from his wounds in steady torrents with every breath he took. Tears filled my eyes. So this was it. Such brains going to waste as a result of the political greed of our leaders! A waste of life, a waste of talent, a waste of potential. How many other Cebos had been killed? What were we becoming if we could snuff the lives of young, talented, educated and productive members of society? What were we doing to ourselves, to our future? Was there a future? And if there was what did it hold for me? Would I live long enough to see a peaceful nation emerge? We had chanted about the need to turn our guns into ploughshares, yet the reality before me made a mockery of this noble dream. Who was to blame? Of course the root cause of it all was apartheid. But were we now so weak we did not realise who was tearing us apart, turning brother against brother?

I knew that Cebo had become a serious fighter. He had been sucked into the maelstrom of this hidden war like so many other people his age. Lying there, unmoving, Cebo's face was suddenly suffused by a beatific smile, and I remembered times when his eyes, now just slits in his face, had been full of mirth. He tried to move his hand, he tried to cough. Blood exploded in crimson spurts.

"*Ya, bangitholile namhlanje, mf'ethu,*" he whispered. Yes, they've got me today, brother.

Somebody attempted to move him, but Cebo half groaned, half laughed, "Tee-he-he, they really got me. Touch My Blood. He-he-he . . . Touch My Blood . . ."

I touched him, held his hands. He was in a bad way, had lost a lot of blood and his chest and rib cage were shattered.

"*Ngishayeni, baf'ethu! Ngishayeni, baf'ethu! Kubuhlungu ukuphefumula!*" he said, his voice faint. Shoot me, brothers, shoot me, brothers. It's getting more painful to breathe.

Cebo's grip tightened, and he died. I knew I had to get away from the madness.

# Epilogue

IT'S 21 MAY 2005. We are seated on benches, on upturned oil drums, on bricks, on grass mats outside my parents' house in Mpumalanga. A fire is going in a corner of the yard. The smells of cooking hang in the warm Durban air. My father is sitting on his haunches with a group of his friends, eating meat. My mother is moving in and out of the house, serving people. She loves working, even when it's not necessary. All these years she has been a domestic worker for various families and a day doesn't end without her making a remark about her work, yet, at fifty-nine, she still refuses to retire. She doesn't need to work as most of her children are grown up, but she won't hear a word about retirement. I tell her to sit down now, and let her daughters do the serving. She just shakes her head, she is the hostess. She is a strong, steadfast woman. Strong both physically and spiritually. She is the person who has inspired most of us to work hard.

I move out of the kitchen and go outside to join my friends. We are sitting in a corner eating meat and drinking beer. Children run about the yard, laughing and screaming. Birds twitter among the branches of my father's favourite avocado tree. The atmosphere is as festive as if we're having a party or enjoying ourselves at a wedding ceremony.

In fact we've just returned from the graveyard where we buried my youngest brother, Thabo Cornelius. He died on 15 May, on what would have been his thirty-second birthday.

Last night, at the vigil, witness after witness testified about how relieved they were that Thabo had not died a sad bloody death like many of his and my peers, our neighbours. He did not die in a hail of police bullets like his friend Fana, who died six years ago while running away from police after having "hit a score" – robbing a Fidelity Guards van. Nor did my brother die at the hands of rival gangs. He died peacefully. He died of AIDS.

It is no longer taboo to mention an AIDS death in the community. It's become so commonplace. We have mourned his death. Now, we are sitting on our haunches, eating meat. We are celebrating his life. Celebrating the fond memories he has left us; celebrating the stories that are now being told about his escapades. He was far more colourful and adventurous than the rest of us. He'd been arrested for hijacking a car when it was still considered a "big, dangerous crime". These days, hijacking is considered an initiation into the life of crime. He also played soccer at second-division level. But now he is dead. We are eating meat in his name.

The ritual of eating meat is accompanied by story telling. The meat goes down well to stories seasoned with dark humour, hyperbole. Each story leads to the next, and before we know it, my friends are telling stories of our childhood. We recall those who died during the political violence, tell of those languishing in jail. Friends who, like Thabo, moved from being angry young men involved in a political war to being cold-hearted bank robbers and hijackers, moulded into fighters by the fires that raged in our townships during the dark days.

In good humour we point out what useless cowards we were not to go down that route. We are not angels, we admit. As we sit here eating meat, we are a human salad of curious characters: some of us never finished school, others are now drunkards who perform odd chores in exchange for beer money. Some of us are drug peddlers. Others are freelance drivers – always willing to be the drivers of getaway cars whenever there is a score in town. Of course others are graduates with good jobs and families to take care of. This is the community we've always been. It does feel uncomfortable eating meat from the same tray as a car hijacker, a man with blood on his hands, but then he is a brother. Every family has its own dark sheep.

People tell their stories of difficulty and say I am lucky, I have a job and a home. I have a wife and children. As a journalist with a senior position, I have the perfect life. I tell them it hasn't been easy. In fact there have been times I've needed to consult a psychiatrist. I encourage them to do the same if they are unable to cope. They laugh because they think it's a joke. Why would a young person go to a psychiatrist? Why would I talk about these things at all, it is just not done. It is while we are talking about psychiatry that someone mentions Mafika Gwala – "your crazy friend", as they call him. They've never been able to understand the man. Not so many people can understand the headspace of true artists. How can one so educated dress the way he does, drink the way he does, live the way he does? they ask. They tell me how unhealthy he is looking now. I make a mental note to visit him. The last time I saw him, a couple of years back, he wasn't well. He had been drinking too much. He had become forgetful and couldn't remember the names of some of our former comrades. He hadn't written anything of substance in years. I wondered how an artist like him could live without indulging in his art. What a waste of talent.

For so many of us the past is a place of hurt, and, in a sense, this book is my own private Truth and Reconciliation Commission. I've tried to account for what I did, and had done to me. I've tried to make peace with that which I cannot change about myself. I survived the old country and belong to the new one. I am grateful for that. Many did not make it.

But this new country is challenging. It might be a country full of hope, but I feel pain when I see the young generation, meaner, more lost than ever we were. But I put aside these thoughts on this hot day with all these characters milling about the yard where I grew up. I am proud to be among people who've known me from childhood, people who have impacted on my life and made me who I am today. I drink to them.